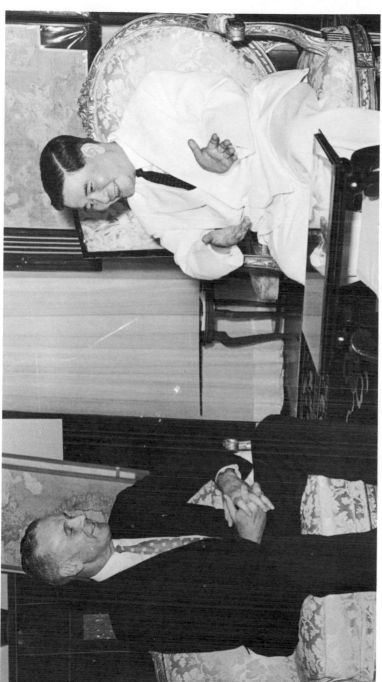

President Diem talks to General Taylor

THE LAST OF THE
MANDARINS:
DIEM
OF VIETNAM

THE LAST OF THE
MANDARINS:
DIEM
OF VIETNAM

by
Anthony Trawick Bouscaren

DUQUESNE UNIVERSITY PRESS, Pittsburgh, Penna.

EDITIONS E. NAUWELAERTS, Louvain

1965

TABLE OF CONTENTS

CHAPTER ONE
NGO DINH DIEM

Ngo Dinh Diem

On November 6th, 1964, Frederick E. Nolting Jr. wrote a letter to the editor of the *New York Times*. This is what he said:

I cannot let this month pass without paying my respects to the memory of a brave man who died for his country a year ago—Ngo Dinh Diem, former President of the Republic of Vietnam.

Events in Vietnam since his overthrow and assassination last November throw light upon some of the problems he faced during his eight years as President of that turbulent country. His Government's achievements under difficult conditions— schools, roads, hospitals, airstrips, land reform, the creation of defense forces and instilling the will to resist—still stand as major obstacles to Communist victory there.

The death of Ngo Dinh Diem casts a long shadow over his troubled land—a shadow that reaches far beyond his own country. But Diem was a patriot, and I am sure that his wish for his people now, as it was throughout the years I knew him, is for their success in their struggle for national survival, political progress, and human dignity.

The tragedy took place in the subtropical greenery of Southeast Asia, but it conveyed some of the pity and terror of the ancient Greek stage. A national hero, who had fought long and courageously against great odds, had finally been brought down by fate - fate in this case being a combination of his avowed enemies, his former friends and, undoubtedly, his own flawed nature. When he took office nine years ago, Ngo Dinh Diem told his people, "Follow me if I advance! Kill me if I retreat! Revenge me if I die!" In whatever manner and for whatever reason Diem died, it was not because he retreated.

Ngo Dinh Diem was a stocky (5 ft. 4 in., 143 lbs.), youngish looking man of 62, with thick black hair and a penchant for white Western-style sharkskin suits. He lived an austere existence. He slept on a monastic narrow cot, protected by a mosquito net and cooled from the tropical heat only by a ceiling fan. He rose every morning at 6:30 a.m., prayed briefly in his private chapel, and then breakfasted on a soup of noodles and chopped pork. After dressing, he received his personal staff at 7:30 a.m. to discuss the day's agenda, then read newspapers and wire reports with great sensitivity to criticism. After a daily physical check-up, he signed state papers and conferred with ranking officers, seated in armchairs in his austere bedroom.

At 1:00 p.m. President Diem lunched alone, and then retired for a siesta until 2:30 p.m. The afternoon was usually spent with visitors, in his office. The beleaguered man sat surrounded with a few intimate possessions - a wooden crucifix, a picture of the Blessed Mother, and hundreds of books on political philosophy and social justice. Diem invariably talked more than he listened, chain-smoked and discoursed volubly. He dined at 8:30 p.m., again usually alone, and then from 9:00 p.m. to 1:00 a.m. conferred with his official family, particularly his brother Nhu.

At the beginning, few thought Diem would last nine months, much less nine years. The Geneva partition of 1954 condemned Viet Nam to be divided into a Communist state in the north and a state of almost total anarchy in the south. The capital city of Saigon was run by bandits. Control of the countryside was split among the private armies of two religious sects and almost anyone else who had a gun.

Into this seemingly doomed situation stepped a scholarly, courageous and principled man of 53, "the most respected and the most influential nationalist leader."[1] Philippe Devillers, probably the most competent historian of contemporary Vietnam, says Diem "was known for his perfect integrity, his competence and intelligence."[2] A convinced nationalist and a practicing Catholic, Ngo Dinh Diem came from a mandarin family long accustomed to rule. Diem himself nearly became a priest but decided against it because, says his brother, Archbishop Thuc, "the church was too worldly for him."

So was nearly everything else. Because he distrusted their motives, Diem refused his support to the French colonialists, the Japanese invaders and the local Communists. He went into self-exile in the U.S. and Belgium, living in Catholic

[1]Paul Mus, *Vietnam: Sociologie d'une guerre* (Paris: Editions du Seuil, 1952), p. 166.
[2]*Histoire du Vietnam de 1940 a 1952* (Paris: Editions du Seuil, 1952), p. 63.

religious communities. In 1954, needing a scape-
goat for their collapsing policies in Asia, France
offered Diem the premiership of South Viet Nam.

All his early opponents underestimated him.
An army commander, who boasted that he had
only to lift a phone to stage a coup, soon found
himself out of a job and out of the country.
Playboy Emperor Bao Dai challenged Diem at
the polls, and found his throne voted out of
existence by 98% of the citizens. Diem smashed
the gangsters who ran Saigon and routed the
armies of the religious sects - with the help of
the general who was later to supplant him. He
also launched a comprehensive land reform program and, on a grass-roots tour of central Viet
Nam in 1954, was nearly trampled by thousands
of wildly cheering peasants. This high point of
his reign was never matched again.

Diem's virtues of honesty, courage and bone-
deep anti-Communism remained. But his faults—
stubbornness, suspicion, a mandarin pride —
became magnified.

Diem was a curious personality, "shy and imposing, congenial and reserved, with clouds of
dreams floating throughout his hardest decisions
in spite of the dreams. *Courage,* of a kind rare
among political leaders, was the outstanding
virtue of the family. Diem's fortitude, once a
course had been set, was unflinching and never
lacking in integrity. He never failed to give
anyone, even his enemies, a fair chance. He
never ordered the death of those who tried to
murder him. He was a good man."[3]

In 1957 President Diem sent the following
message to a conference of American friends

[3]Suzanne Labin, *Vietnam, An Eye-Witness Account*
Springfield, Va.: Crestwood Books, 1964), p. 64.

of Vietnam in Washington, D.C., pleading for understanding and support:

It is heartening to know that friends such as you have gathered in your capital city across the world from us to spend a day on Vietnamese affairs. The very name of your group is warming, for we have learned to trust the Americans. We need true friends today.

There are still people who hope for our failure. Some because they have predicted it, others because of ideology and an absence of fighting spirit, want us to appease our enemies with our birthright as free men. Some spread malicious falsehoods about the state of our nation, because, fearing that they might compromise themselves and despairing for its recovery, they have not participated in its restoration. But the strength of our friendship with you is the strength of truth. Let this be known.

It is true that much has been done in recent months. But it is also true that we have arrived at a critical point in our national life. It would be tempting to rest now. While other Asian countries less threatened than ours took five to ten years to develop democratic institutions, we have in one year established an independent republic, elected an assembly of free men to write a constitution, ended the armed threat of feudalistic forces, united all of our free people except a handful who want the overwhelming majority to concede to their selfish dictates, established effective government throughout the land. Where previous governments have dared not venture, such as in the Plaine des Joncs, we are opening vast new opportunities to millions of people, settling hundreds of thousands of refugees on productive land.

This is just a beginning. Freedom is not gained nor held so soon. We are aware that our brothers in the North have been enslaved by the Communists, mobilized in millions to labor for a foreign ideology, and impressed into an army so huge that their masters must keep a sinister silence about why it is so huge. We know that we must work to obtain our freedom and work hard and with discipline.

We must now give more meaning to our hard sought liberty. The sovereignty to our citizens must be brought to rewarding life through the constitution. The richness of our land must be made to bear fuller sustenance for all our people who have known years of warfare. To attain that goal, we need technicians and machines. Our armed forces which are considerably reduced must however undertake an immense task from the military as well as the cultural and social point of view. It is indispensable that our army have the wherewithal to become increasingly capable of preserving the peace which we seek. There are an infinite number of tasks in all fields to complete before the year's end. Economic aid can be only effective once security has been restored.

We must become a strong free people, with beliefs and institutions so precious to us that we will willingly risk life itself to defend them. To do this, we count on your friendship, that is to say, on your effort to understand us.

Please continue to encourage us.

Among those in the audience was Senator John F. Kennedy.

Following Diem's death, General Thomas Lane made this evaluation:

It is said that President Diem was difficult to deal with. So is President de Gaulle,
so was Chancellor Adenauer, so are all
men who are too noble to be puppets. It
used to be the hope of the United States to
see men of high character and ability
raised to leadership among our allies. It
is not so any longer.

In eight years of remarkable achievement under President Diem, the people of
South Vietnam secured their independence
and achieved unity beyond the most san-
guine expectations of 1956. Through the
strategic-hamlet program of concentrating
the peasants in fortified villages for self-
defense, they have protected seventy-five
percent of the people and of the national
area from the dominion and terror of the
Viet Cong. Completion of the program
in another year or two seemed assured.

In the fortified villages, new standards
of democracy were established. Peasants
had their first experience of self-government
in the election of village officials. A million
additional peasants have been brought into
the village system within the past year.

Solution of the great economic and military problems of South Vietnam required a
national discipline which the Diem leadership provided.

The effective and vigorous prosecution
of the war effort by President Diem has
been attested by all competent military
observers. Fine teamwork with U.S. military advisors had been developed and
efficient national military forces had been
created. What then was the U.S. criticism
of President Diem? Did we take a few riots
stimulated by Communist agents as evidence that he lacked public support? Did
the opposition of a tiny fraction of the

nation's Buddhists, some of whom had fought with Ho-Chi-Minh against the French, convince us that a better leadership could be found? Was President Diem a tyrant who practiced terror?

President Diem enjoyed the full faith and confidence of the country people. In the cities, however, where corruption and intrigue had long held sway before he came to power, his police necessarily kept a careful monitorship of hostile forces. Even with these, his Administration was one of mildness and concern. The Buddhist leaders apprehended for insurrection, the student riot leaders, were not bludgeoned with Castro-type cruelty. They were re-educated in loyalty to the nation and released as fast as their future good behavior could be expected. So, too, prisoners taken from the Viet Cong were educated for return to a free society. These actions reflected President Diem's wisdom and his solicitude for all his people. There was paternalism, but no terror, in the Diem Government.

Now the President is dead. There can be no doubt that he was murdered by those who accepted his surrender. The treacherous General Minh and Vice President Tho are not big enough men to have faced the President they betrayed. It was necessary to arrange his execution to avoid such a confrontation. While he lived, the people would not accept the rebel leaders.[4]

Even his enemies will admit, in a calmer moment, that had it not been for the stubbornness and courage of this diffidently shy aristo-

[4]General Thomas A. Lane, "A Black Day In Our History": Syracuse *Post Standard*, Nov. 5, 1963

crat, South Viet Nam today might be under the iron rule of Communism.

No one may ever know his last words or thoughts. To judge from the record of his life, he must have felt betrayed, and convinced to the end that he was right.

"History may yet adjudge Diem as one of the great figures of the Twentieth Century."[5]

[5]William Henderson, "South Vietnam Finds Itself", *Foreign Affairs*, January, 1957, p. 285

CHAPTER TWO
BOYHOOD TO
JAPANESE OCCUPATION

Boyhood to Japanese Occupation

The term "Mandarin" applies to the old-style civil servants of the Annamese Emperors who once ruled Indo-China. Like the British district officers in colonial India, mandarins wandered about their dominions like small potentates. Besides overseeing such matters as the collection of taxes, they settled all manner of village disputes, in the name of the government. In time, a good mandarin came to know the people intimately, and became a father image in the rice-growing hamlets under his charge. Such a background shaped the personality of Ngo Dinh Diem, first President of the Republic of Vietnam, and father of his country.

Until 1943, the French Government-General in Indo-China published every year a book, always bound in red, which was a sort of Who's Who of Political leaders in Cambodia, Laos and Vietnam. Among those included were Princes Boun Oum, Souvanna Phouma, and Souphanouvong of Laos, Princes Norodom Sihanouk and Monireth of Cambodia, and such diverse Vietnamese leaders as Pham Van Dong and Tran Van Huu. The Ngo family was also well represented in the last editions: Archbishop

11

Ngo Dinh Thuc, and a young intellectual who had graduated from France's famous Ecole des Chartes—Ngo Dinh Nhu; another brother, Ngo Dinh Khoi, was listed as a *tong-doc,* a provincial governor in the administration of the French protectorate of Annam. Three of the Ngo brothers, however, were missing in that array of native leaders whom the French considered actually or potentially important. One of them was Jean-Baptiste Ngo Dinh Diem.

In his book, *The Two Viet-Nams,* Bernard Fall writes: "It is to say the least, remarkable that Ngo Dinh Diem has thus far escaped the attentions of a biographer." It is remarkable indeed.

In the days when the kingdom of Annam, in the central section of Vietnam, was independent—and even after it became a French protectorate, in 1883—it was ruled by a succession of emperors, whose palace was in the imperial city of Hue, on the coast of the South China Sea four hundred miles north of the Republic of Vietnam's present capital, Saigon. In Hue, on January 3, 1901, Ngo Dinh Kha, a high-ranking mandarin, soon to be court chamberlain in the retinue of the Emperor Thanh Thai, became the father of the third of the six sons he ultimately sired. To the infant's family name of Ngo were added the middle name of Dinh and the given name of Diem.

Ngo Dinh Diem is generally referred to in Vietnam by his given name — Diem — which means burning jade, but it is also proper to call him by his family name – Ngo. He was born on January 3, 1901 in a straw hut on his father's estate near Hue. Diem comes from a clan of leaders who for 1,000 years defended the Vietnamese against invaders from China. In the seventeenth century the Ngo Dinh clan was converted to Catholicism, and they held to their faith at a grisly price: as recently as 1870, no fewer than one-hundred of the Ngo Dinh were surrounded in their church and burned alive.

Persecution of Catholics began in earnest in the 1830s, with savage beatings and dismemberment the favored tactics of Emperor Minh Mang. Then in 1848 and 1851 Emperor Tu Duc issued edicts leading to the terrorization of Catholics and more massacres.

Diem's father, one of the clan's few survivors, was a mandarin first class (a kind of Grand Vizier) at the court of Emperor Than Thai (who reigned from 1889 to 1907), wearing the traditional silken robes and two-inch fingernails. Ngo Dinh Kha was a towering figure in the imperial court, and one of Vietnam's foremost educators. He personally supervised the education of his nine children. Each morning he took all the children to six o'clock Mass; later, in the rose garden, he would give his third son Diem some extra tuition — working in the rice paddies with the peasants. "A man must understand the life of a farmer," father Kha explained.

Ngo Dinh Kha had been Minister of Rites and Grand Chamberlain to Emperor Than-Thai; he had conceived a deep resentment against the French when they deposed his sovereign. Ngo Kinh Kha resigned his government positions, cut himself off from all unessential contacts with the French, and began to support such Vietnamese nationalist reformers as Phan Boi Chau (1867-1940), who became Vietnam's Sun-Yat-sen and founder of the first nationalist groups organized along Western lines.

Diem took to this austerity, got up at 5:00 a.m. to study, and prayed two hours every day. At the age of six, he won his first school prize for "assiduousness," a trait that turned out to be deeply ingrained in his character. "When there were floods," recalls one of his brothers, "father would make us stay home. The rest of us loved it, but Diem would sneak off along the dikes and go to school just the same." When he returned home, no sense that any injustice was being done, Diem would accept his father's whipping for disobedience.

Ngo Dinh Kha passed on to his sons, particularly the older Khoi and Diem, his ardent nationalism and deep religious faith. Diem adopted his father's rigid antagonism toward the foreign occupiers of his country. When his father retired to his farm holdings rather than collaborate with the French, young Diem was left at Hue, in the care of the imperial court's Premier, Nguyon Huu Bai, who, in the traditional Vietnamese fashion, reared him as his son and prevailed upon him to seek an administrative career in spite of the hated French - for only service in the colonial administration would provide the future independent Vietnam with cadres familiar with the intricacies of modern government.

His formal schooling was twice interrupted - once in 1908, when the French replaced the Emperor Thanh Thai with a more tractable puppet, putting the court chamberlain out of work for several months before he came back into favor, and again when, at fifteen, the boy spent a few months in a monastery, only to decide that the priesthood was not for him. Nevertheless, at sixteen he was ready to take the competitive examinations for the equivalent of a high school diploma.   He scored so well that the French Government offered him a scholarship in Paris, but he declined.   But even then, he had a burning ambition to work for Vietnamese independence, and he did not want to lose his chance. "Those of us who did go to France came back a mixture of many things," another brother said, "but Diem is pure Vietnamese."

Having completed his lycee studies at Hue (the same place that Ho Chi Minh had studied ten years earlier), Diem entered the French-run School for Law and Administration at Hanoi. An intense debater and an excellent student as well Diem succeeded brilliantly.   He graduated in 1921 at the top of his class of twenty, and immediately entered the provincial administration as a district chief.   He moved ahead so rapidly that by the time he reached his mid-twenties he had attained a mandarinic rank entitling him to the use of a rickshaw and a span of coolies and was the administrative supervisor of a region embracing three hundred villages in the general vicinity of Hue — a job in which he acted not only as tax collector and director of public works but as both sheriff and judge in settling disputes among the peasants. Wearing a conical straw hat and mandarin robe, and traveling on horseback rather than in his rickshaw, he diligently made the rounds of his bailiwick, and what he learned in the course of these journeys prompted him to recommend to the French authorities that the villages be granted greater autonomy and better educational facilities.   The French authorities ignored him.   In 1925, or thereabouts, he became one of the first Vietnamese officials to learn of the Communists' designs on the country when, at Quang Tri, sixty miles north of Hue, he came across evidence of underground activity on the part of Ho Chi Minh, who was eventually to rule Communist North Vietnam but was then just a party organizer. Diem made a study of Communism and sent agents to infiltrate the cells that Ho was setting up, with the result that, in 1929, when the Communists staged public demonstrations all over the country, the young mandarin was well prepared to round up the leaders of the movement in his administrative area, and swiftly did so.[1]

He paraded the more arrogant Communists in rags and told the villagers: "They say they stand for the poor people... well, let them dress like it." But Diem was no lackey of the French; from the very start he was the first leader of the free Vietnamese to oppose French rule and fight for freedom. In 1929, at the early age of twenty-eight, he was appointed governor of Phan-Thiet, the province and city in which Ho Chi Minh had taught school previously. As senior official in a province that included lowland Vietnamese as well as mountaineers and remnants of the Cham minorities, Ngo Dinh Diem did an excellent job. He judged fairly, was known not to take bribes, and "even then fought the revolutionary ideas the young firebrands of the Than-Nien were bringing back from Hong Kong, Canton, and Saigon."[2] Not that Diem favored collaboration with the French, for this was the

---

[1] Robert Shaplen, "A Reporter in Vietnam", *New Yorker*, September 22, 1962, p. 103.

[2] Bernard Fall, *The Two Viet-Nams* (New York: Praeger, 1963), p. 239.

farthest thing from his mind; but he was against the kind of revolution that would not only sweep away the French but uproot traditionalism and the mystique of Vietnam. He was, in short, more in the tradition of the American revolution (actually a war of liberation) than of the French revolution.

By 1932, Diem's reputation as an able and energetic administrator had filtered back to the imperial capital, where young Emperor Bao Dai, aflame with the modern ideas he had brought back from France, wanted to reform his archaic administration.

After the failure of the Communist-inspired revolutionary movements during 1933, "A Catholic mandarin, thirty-two years old, reputed for his complete integrity, Ngo Dinh Diem, then Governor of Phan Thiet, was offered the Interior Ministry and the Secretariat of the Commission on Reforms." [3] All about him he saw the poverty of his people, their lack of opportunity, the shameful treatment of foreign rule. Accordingly, he drew up a list of reforms, designed to pave the way for self-government. But Ngo Dinh Diem fell out with his sovereign and the French when it became apparent that the latter would not agree to endow Annam's Chamber of People's Representatives with effective legislative powers. "True to his reputation for 'all-or-nothing' integrity, he resigned in July after having publicly accused the Emperor of being 'nothing but an instrument in the hands of the French authorities,' and handed back all the titles

[3] Philippe Devillers, *Histoire du Vietnam de 1940 a 1952* (Paris: Editions du Seuil, 1952), p. 63.

and decorations bestowed on him by Bao Dai and the French." [4]

Like his father before him, Ngo Dinh Diem now retired from public view for almost a decade, to devote his time to study and reading. But he maintained intense correspondence with Vietnamese nationalist leaders, such as Phan Boi Chau and Prince Cuong-De, and his house became a regular rendezvous for anti-French and anti-Communist nationalists.

Diem spent the next seven years in passive resistance to French rule, striving meanwhile to build up a non-Communist freedom movement. Although the French helped to develop the resources of Vietnam and brought treasures of culture to the country, they missed few chances to turn an extra franc. Salt workers were compelled to sell to the French, who sold it back to the Vietnamese at higher prices. Each village had its alcohol quota, a specific amount, based on population, to be bought from the French-controlled sources. "I saw the danger from the Communists," said Ngo Dinh Diem, "and I could see how they would exploit such injustices. We had to have democratic reforms, or it was clear even then that the Communists would win."

During World War II, Communist leader Nguyen Ai Quoc took the name Ho Chi Minh. He and his Vietminh organization received a shot in the arm in the form of American aid - mostly weapons from the OSS (Office of Strategic Services). This in return for informations about the Japanese which, "although frequently

4Fall, *op. cit.*, p. 239.

not very exact... had the merit of being numerous, and this always makes an impression."[5]

From the outset Ho Chi Minh set out to woo the Americans. Several OSS teams provided the Vietminh guerrillas with American arms and ammunition. OSS missions operating in North Vietnam and even China acquired a number of Vietnamese aides, many of whom turned out to be Vietnamese Communists. When Ho's forces took over Hanoi, the presence of American senior officers at Vietminh functions and the flying of the American flag over their residence made it easy to convince the unsophisticated population (and even the surviving French who began to emerge slowly from their various internment camps) that the United States had established official relations with the Vietminh regime and was giving the revolutionaries its fullest backing. Later, it was learned that the belief in Ho's American backing led Bao-Dai and his nationalist supporters to abandon the reins of government to the Vietminh without a struggle.[6]

The Vietminh used their main weapon—terror—not only in isolated attacks on the Japanese, but on more frequent attacks on non-Communist Vietnamese nationalist opponents.

During the war and its aftermath, the Japanese, the French, and Ho Chi Minh's Communists all fought one another for Indo-China; all three wanted support from Nationalist Diem. But Diem rejected collaboration of any sort; he told the Japanese: "Why should I join you, who enslave my country? I will one day lead a free

[5]Philippe Devillers, "Vietnamese Nationalism and French Politics," in *Asian Nationalism and the West*, edited by William L. Holland, New York, 1953, p. 106.

[6]Fall, *op. cit.*, pp. 100, 101.

people."[7]   He spent much of the time in Hue, at the home of a younger brother, Ngo Dinh Can, who was then a fledgling worker in the nationalist cause, and who later dominated the region of Hue politically and economically.   In Hue, Diem went to Mass every morning, and passed the rest of the day either reading or engaging in one of his four hobbies, which he still pursued when he had the chance - riding, hunting, gardening, and photography.   From time to time, he travelled south to Saigon, where he met with other nationalists and intellectuals to discuss a possible revolution.   He had no specific plans, no organization, and not much personal following.   On one occasion, he met Vo Nguyen Giap, who later became the chief of the Viet Cong, or Communist, forces in South Vietnam, but who was then a Left Wing Socialist, and during a long conversation each man tried unsuccessfully to convert the other.   The French were obviously keeping Diem under surveillance, and at one point they warned him that he was undermining the position of one of his older brothers—Ngo Dinh Khoi, who was governor of Quang Nam province, south of Hue — simply by visiting him now and then. Whether for that reason or some other, Khoi was forced to resign from the French administration in 1942.

By 1942, the Japanese had completed the occupation of Vietnam, which they had begun in 1940— without, however, interfering particularly with the French administration.   Diem sounded out a number of the higher-ups among the newcomers on the possibility of creating a free nation under their auspices, but with a war on their

[7]O.K. Armstrong, "Biggest Little Man in Asia," *Readers Digest*, February, 1956.

hands the Japanese had other, more pressing matters to think about. So Diem resumed his placid way of life, except that now, instead of visiting Khoi, he made an occasional trip south to see another older brother, Archbishop Ngo Dinh Thuc, who lived near Saigon. Then, one day in the summer of 1944, as Diem was returning from a walk through the streets of Hue, he noticed a bustle in the neighborhood of Can's house and, suspecting — correctly — that the French had come to arrest him, slipped away and spent the night in the home of a friend who lived nearby. The next day, the French officially declared him to be a subversive influence, and put his name on a wanted list. Diem fled south to Saigon, where he found sanctuary in the homes of friends.

The end of World War II and the defeat of Japan ushered in not peace, but a new war: a war launched by the International Communist movement in East Asia. While the French and Americans celebrated the defeat of Japan, Communists in China and Indo-China consolidated their positions, and with Soviet aid began to systematically attack anti-Communist groups, and leaders.

Early in 1945 Ho's Communist troops struck at the nationalist Ngo Dinh clan, raiding the mansion at Hue and burning Diem's collection of 10,000 books. They took hold of Diem's respected elder brother, Ngo Dinh Khoi and his eldest son, dragged them out of their home and whisked them away in a green citroen to the village of Co Bi, in the high jagged mountains of the Chaine Mystique where both were murdered. Diem himself barely escaped with his own life, and said of his brother: "He was the brightest son of our family, a tall handsome man. The

21

welfare of his people was his life's work."[8]   Nine
years later Khoi's body and that of his son were
found, after the Communists had been driven
out of the area.

The collapse of Japanese power left Saigon
to the mercies of the murderous Viet Minh bands
of Tran Van Giau.   Hue, where Bao Dai had
surrendered to the Viet Minh, seemed the most
likely haven of peace to Diem.   But at the same
time that Diem slipped out of Saigon and set out
for Hue along the dusty coastal road, his brother
Nhu left Hue on foot to escape probable seizure
in the Viet Minh-occupied imperial capital.   Nhu
finally made Saigon safely, but Diem never
reached Hue.   Recognized and seized by the Viet
Minh in the little fishing port of Tuy-Hoa, Diem
was manhandled and dragged north to Ho Chi
Minh's mountain stronghold at Tuyen-Quang.
He was first exposed to the perils of illness and
hunger in the Tonkinese mountains, and then
was taken to Hanoi, where Ho Chi Minh tried to
persuade him to enter his government: "Come
and live with me in the palace," he said.   Diem
replied: "You killed my brother.   You are a
criminal."   Ho protested: "I know nothing about
your brother... You are upset and angry.   Stay
with me.   We must all work together against the
French."   The future President of his country then
declared: "I don't believe you understand the
kind of man I am.   Look me in the face.   Am I
a man who fears?"   Ho looked and then said
"No."   "Good.   Then I will go now," retorted
Diem.   Ho let him go.   Diem's two dominant
traits — "stubborn courage and, even more un-

8 *Time*, February 27, 1956, p. 36.

shakable, family solidarity" — clearly showed themselves in this exchange. [9]

On March 9th, 1945, Emperor Bao Dai was confronted with a Japanese coup d'etat at Hue. The Japanese Ambassador informed him that Vietnam was now free, and urged Bao Dai to stay on as Chief of State and help Japan in the building of a Greater East Asia. The Emperor decided he had no other choice, and on March 11th, he announced to the people that Vietnam was independent. After the Japanese coup, Bao Dai's cabinet split on what course it ought to follow. It finally decided that all its members should resign, in favor of a new, more representative government. When the cabinet was dissolved, popular demonstrations broke out in Hue in favor of Ngo Dinh Diem. Bao Dai sent a telegram to Diem, then living in Saigon, inviting him to become Prime Minister. But Diem was convinced, most recently by the actions of the then French Commissioner, Admiral Jean Decoux, that collaboration with France was incompatible with freedom. Nor were the Japanese, who remained in effective control of Vietnam, anxious to have Ngo Dinh Diem lead the new government. He wanted a real independence and unity for the country which they were not prepared to give, but which they would have found politically awkward to refuse when requested by a man as popular among the Vietnamese as he was. According to reliable sources, it is believed that Bao Dai's telegram to Diem was never delivered because of Japanese interference. [10]

[9] Fall, *op. cit.*, p. 241.
[10] Ellen J. Hammer, *The Struggle for Indo-China*, (Stanford, Stanford University Press, 1954), p. 48.

Ngo Dinh Diem, for his part, knowing that the Japanese were not prepared to make radical changes in the status of the country, made no effort to seek office under Bao Dai. The upshot was that the Emperor finally asked a respected old scholar and prominent Freemason, Tran Trong Kim to take the job, and Kim became Prime Minister in April. But independence under the new regime was in name only. The Japanese were really in charge. Some elements in and around the Kim Government were Communist and pro-Communist, and Kim told a visitor in June that he was prepared to hand power over to the Vietminh. But the Communists were awaiting for Japan to capitulate before moving in from the sidelines. [11]

[11]*Ibid.*, p. 150.

CHAPTER THREE
NEITHER FRANCE
NOR COMMUNISM

Neither France Nor Communism

The refusal of Ngo Dinh Diem to accede to the wishes of Bao Dai in March, 1945, in spite of popular demonstrations for him in Hue, increased his stature among non-Communist Vietnamese nationalists. "It is part of Ngo Dinh Diem's political greatness not to have succumbed to the deceptive magic of unity, to have refused to enter into it with elements of national disruption..." [1]

In 1946 Admiral Thierry d'Argenlieu was appointed by De Gaulle as High Commissioner for France in Indo-China. He tried to win over nationalist moderates for a Vietnamese government ready to cooperate with the French. He approached Ngo Dinh Diem, but refused to meet Diem's conditions. In the view of the French, "there could be no question for the civil services and the French government of admitting a leader of a united Vietnam like Ngo Dinh Diem ...whose nationalism frightened them." [2]

[1] Joseph Buttinger, in Richard Lindholm, Ed., *Vietnam, The First Five Years* (Ann Arbor: University of Michigan Press, 1959), pp. 43, 30.
[2] Philippe Devillers, "Vietnamese Nationalism and French Politics," in *Asian Nationalism and the West,* edited by William L. Holland, New York 1953, p. 396.

A few weeks after the Japanese surrender (August, 1945), Ho Chi Minh set up his own regime, called the Viet Minh, in Hanoi, and early in 1946 Ho made a deal with the French, whereby, at least for the time being, they accepted his northern regime.

Early in 1946 Diem was almost captured by the Communists in Hanoi, and found refuge in a monastery run by some Canadian monks. He continued to elude the Communists, and tried to stir up nationalist, anti-Communist sentiment in the north. Meantime Ho Chi Minh went to Paris in the autumn of 1946 for further negotiations with the French, but as these achieved nothing, war between the Vietminh and the French became inevitable. As fighting broke out in the north, Diem made his way south, and spent much of 1947 living with his brother, Bishop Ngo Dinh Thuc, near Saigon.

Up to this time Diem's "undeviating adherence to his principles had been making him more and more of a lone wolf."[3] "Playing again on an 'all or nothing basis'", Diem remained aloof both from the French regime in Saigon-Hue and the Vietminh in Hanoi, and created in South and Central Vietnam a small political party with a name that in itself was a program: Phong Trao Quoc-Gia Qua Kich, or Nationalist Extremist Movement. This group advocated resistance both to the French and the Vietminh, but it never amounted to very much.[4] He did succeed in putting out newspapers in both Saigon and Hanoi (from which the French had in the interim driven out the Communists), but the French suppressed his party and his newspapers. But these

[3]Shaplen, *op. cit.,* p. 115.
[4]Fall, *op. cit.,* p. 241.

ventures did make Diem better known throughout Vietnam, as a principled and courageous
nationalist who would accept nothing short of
dominion status for Vietnam within the French
Union, an association of states patterned after
the British Commonwealth.

Now the French again turned to Emperor
Bao Dai (who was in Hong Kong since the
Japanese surrender), seeking to find popular
support for him among Vietnamese nationalists.
"It was necessary to find a way of giving Bao
Dai a 'democratic' appearance, which would per-
mit him to negotiate 'in the name of the Viet-
namese people.'' [5] On December 22, 1947, Bao
Dai invited Diem and other leaders to Hong
Kong, to report on his talks with French High
Commissioner Emile Bollaert (who had suc-
ceeded d'Argenlieu in March). But Diem told
Bao Dai that he considered the concessions the
French were ready to make in behalf of Viet-
namese freedom to be "absolutely insufficient,
incapable of satisfying national aspirations and
therefore re-establishing peace." [6]

The trouble with the French was that after
correctly concluding that it was impossible to do
business with Ho Chi Minh, they failed to make
the necessary concessions to the bona fide nationalists whose accession to power provided the
only possible solution. Nevertheless these
nationalists persisted in their efforts. On February 22nd, 1948, Diem invited Vietnamese
leaders, including those of the religious "sects"
and representatives of the provincial governments in the South, to assemble in Saigon, in
order to discuss the conditions of further negotia-

[5] Devillers, *Histoire du Vietnam, op. cit.,* p. 425.
[6] *Ibid.,* p. 420.

tions with the French. These conditions were that the French must deal with this "Congress of Notables", and accept the representative designated by the Congress as most qualified to lead Vietnam. But High Commissioner Bollaert was evasive. On March 22, 1948, Bollaert told Diem that something comparable to Dominion status for Vietnam was impossible — a condition Diem and his colleagues had insisted on. Two days later, on Diem's initiative, the Congress of Notables adopted a motion to create a Study Committee, leading to the formation of a provisional government of national unity. [7] Diem pointed out that Bao Dai could then have established a truly national government capable of competing with the Vietminh for the loyalties of the people. "But this statesmanlike plan did not appeal to members of Bao Dai's entourage who preferred to see a government established immediately, regardless of its necessarily unrepresentative character." [8]

In June, 1948, both Bao Dai and the French, who were finding the government they had established unworkable, appealed to Diem for advice. He responded by demanding social, economic, and political reforms that went far beyond anything the French were willing to grant. His demands, which he published in the form of a manifesto, consequently fizzled, and he withdrew from the public scene. "The intellectuals in Saigon did a lot of talking about independence, but few of them were brave enough to rally around my program," he said; "They simply went on with petty intrigues of their own, and

[7] *Ibid.,* pp. 425-430.

[8] Eleanor Hammer, *The Struggle for Indochina* (Stanford, Stanford University Press, 1954),p. 219.

accepted Bao Dai to the end." [9]

Again in 1949, the Mandarin of Hue had an opportunity to lead the country, but again, the French insisted on retaining too much power. In that year Bao Dai (no longer Emperor), took on the title "Chief of State", and he invited Diem to become Premier. But Diem declined, asserting: "The national aspirations of the Vietnamese people will be satisfied only on the day when our nation obtains the same political status which India and Pakistan enjoy... I believe it is only just to reserve the best posts in the new Vietnam for those who have merited most of the country: I speak of the resistance elements." [10]

In the spring of 1950, having been informed that the Vietminh had sentenced him to death *in absentia*, he applied to the French for protection only to be told that no police were available for such duty. "Diem had never been one to panic, and this time, too, he made no immediate move, but he must have started wondering whether a live nationalist, however far from his native soil, was not to be preferred to a dead one on it." [11]

In August, 1950, having obtained permission from the French to attend the celebration of the Holy Year in Rome, he headed for Italy, via Japan and the United States. He was accompanied by his brother, Archbishop Thuc. In Japan they visited Diem's old-time ideal of national resistance, Prince Coung-De. In Tokyo, Diem was advised by some members of the American colony to go to the United States to plead for Vietnamese independence. Accordingly Diem and Archbishop Thuc visited the United

[9] Shaplen, p. 116.
[10] *L'Echo du Vietnam,* June 16, 1949.
[11] Shaplen, *op. cit.*

States during September and October, and won many converts to their cause, among them Francis Cardinal Spellman. The brothers then moved on to Rome, for an audience with Pope Pius XII, followed by visits to Switzerland, France, and Belgium, where Diem established contacts with Vietnamese exile groups.

The importance of the United States position on Vietnam was underscored in 1951, when the Truman Administration began to provide the French and Bao Dai with aid against the Vietminh. Ngo Dinh Diem returned to America that year, to plead his cause for a non-French and anti-Communist independence movement. His base in the United States was the Maryknoll Seminary in Ossining, New York, from which he made frequent lecture trips, especially to eastern college audiences. He also visited Washington several times, and succeeded in enlisting the support of Congressman Walter Judd, together with Senators Mike Mansfield and John F. Kennedy.

After spending two years in the United States, Diem went to Belgium, where he took up residence in the Benedictine Monastery of Saint-Andre-les-Bruges, which is also a key center of missionary activities in the Far East. There he became closely associated with Father Raymond de Jaegher, the well-known Belgian authority on Communism in East Asia.

During Diem's absence, Bao Dai three times offered him the Premiership. He rejected the first two offers out of hand because they were hedged with French-inspired restrictions; the third promised him unlimited political authority, but still did not grant his demand that the Vietnamese be allowed to take over the conduct of the war against the Vietminh from the French. "If we had been responsible for prosecuting the war, we would have won," he said. "The Communists were exhausted, and even in some of the northern provinces, where they had been in control for as long as nine years, they did not have the people with them. A majority of Vietnamese would have supported a genuinely independent government, but the French were defeatists in sizing up the real sentiment of the country." [12]

Ngo Dinh Nhu, a trade union leader and brother of Ngo Dinh Diem, assumed a leading role in organizing an unofficial "Congress of National Unity and Peace" in Cholon, on September 6, 1953. It demanded unconditional independence for Vietnam and, on the domestic level, the immediate summoning of a national assembly, freedom of press and association, an end to corruption, and reforms of the army and administration. But the French were not yet prepared to give in. In her book *The Struggle for Indochina,* Eleanor Hammer writes: "In Indochina French policies had long played into the hands of the Communists: by rejecting the idea of independence for any Vietnamese regime, regardless of its politics, French officials for years had made it impossible for the Bao Dai government to have any hope of success against the Viet Minh." [13]

At the beginning of 1954, people in the Free World began to understand the seriousness of the situation in Vietnam. When the French government discovered that the United States was not prepared to intervene to save the situation, it decided to beat a retreat. The Geneva

[12] *Ibid.,* p. 118.
[13] Hammer, *op. cit.,* pp. 305, 306.

Conference opened on April 26, 1954, attended by all the major powers and some smaller ones too. The fall of Dienbienphu on May 6 reduced the influence of those people in France who wanted to continue to struggle for Indo-china; at the same time it strengthened the hand of those in France and elsewhere who had come to believe that a Communist triumph was inevitable. On July 21, the government of Mendes-France signed the historic and fateful Geneva Agreement, which ended the war in Indochina, partitioned Vietnam, and left South Vietnam, Cambodia, and Laos to their fate. Mendes had the same illusions about the Communists that Chamberlain had about the Nazis in 1938. The Geneva agreement was almost a carbon copy of the Panmunjom settlement in Korea.

Dienbienphu was one of the crucial battles of the 20th century. The French lured the Communists into an open battle by occupying the low lands of Dienbienphu. But the French underestimated the capability of the enemy to bring up artillery for the assault. Even then, the situation could have been saved by a resolute French policy or American intervention. The West chose not to act, convinced that a policy of accommodation could buy peace in south-east Asia. The French surrendered the fortress on May 7, 1954, after a siege of 55 days.

But the price of "peace" was high. France had lost her richest colony after having spent over seven billion dollars of her money and more than four billion in American aid; the people of Vietnam were forced to accept the division of their country, and over one million persons were forced to flee north Vietnam; and the nations opposed to the spread of Communism had to now face the extension into north Vietnam of a Communist regime — a colony of the Sino-Soviet Empire. And this was not all. The price of "peace" included a revival of the dreary conviction that the West had no policy to counteract the expansion of Communism in east Asia; the disease of defeatism was on the increase.

Following the fall of Dienbienphu, and the end of French military dominance in Vietnam, and the signing of the final independence accords by Prince Buu-Loc, the way was paved for an honorable return home. While the Geneva Conference was underway, the French agreed, on June 6th, 1954, to the appointment of Ngo Dinh Diem as Premier of South Vietnam, and on June 15th Diem assumed his office as head of the government. As he arrived in Saigon on June 26th, French planes were bringing refugees and wounded into the capital, while other planes were flying north with ammunition and para-troop reinforcements for the last desperate battles of the Indo-china war. On July 7th, Diem formed his first cabinet, and from that time on the "Double Seven" (seventh day of the seventh month) was a holiday in South Vietnam.

The confusion facing the new Premier was staggering. Under the Geneva agreement, the Communists were allowed to remain in certain parts of South Vietnam for ten months, during which time they were supposed to assemble and evacuate their forces; actually, they spent the time spreading suspicion and discontent among the peasants. Fortunately, some of the Redemptorists Fathers set the record straight. At the Geneva Conference, India, Poland, and Canada had been called upon to set up an International Control Commission, which would see to it that the provisions of the settlement were adhered to, and they had duly sent representatives to Vietnam; but since both the Indians and the Poles were hostile to Diem, his complaints about Communist violations of the agreement were largely ignored, leaving the violators free to redouble their mischief-making.

The extent of popular opposition to Viet Minh rule was revealed after the signing of the cease-fire agreement. Although the French authorities anticipated that wealthy Vietnamese, and those who had served the Bao Dai regime would be unlikely to remain in Tongking, the possibility of a massive exodus was discounted. In consequence, the French authorities who had undertaken to evacuate Vietnamese civilians from Tongking estimated that they would be required to provide transport for some 30,000 refugees, but it was soon apparent that this figure represented a gross underestimate. By the beginning of August 70,000 applications for passages to South Vietnam had been received.

Ngo Dinh Diem, who had exhorted the population of North Vietnam in a speech at Hanoi on August 3rd "to rally the South in order to continue the struggle for independence and liberty", [14] then sent a personal message to President Eisenhower requesting American assistance in the evacuation of civilians and an urgent appeal was issued to friendly nations and to international philanthropic organizations for assistance in the provision of relief for the destitute refugees, who were now arriving in large numbers in South Vietnam. The American response was prompt, and orders were immediately given

[14]*LeMonde,* 4 August 1954.

to the Seventh Fleet to sail for Indochina, while an assurance was provided that aid would be forthcoming. [15]

The pitiable condition of most refugees has been described by Dr. Tom Dooley, Father Patrick O'Connor and others. In many cases, the Communists tried to prevent people in the north from leaving, in violation of the Geneva accords. But these crimes against humanity were largely ignored by the "neutral nations" commission of Poland, India and Canada. The partition of Vietnam, like that of Korea and Germany before it, uprooted millions of people, many of whom did not survive the ordeal. But the accommodationists at Geneva apparently did not foresee this.

The fact that all the movement was from north to south pretty well demonstrated how the people, and especially the peasants, felt about the Communist Vietminh. But the problems of resettlement were vast, and the predominantly Catholic refugees often found a cool, or worse, welcome, from Buddhist groups in the south.

Most of the refugees from the north were Catholics. The persecutions and torture to which they were subjected by the Vietminh defies description. On January 22, 1955, Premier Diem declared: "It is my duty to denounce before the free world and before Christendom the inhuman acts of repression and coercion taken by the Vietminh against populations wanting to leave the Communist zone, acts which are flagrant violations of the Geneva agreement."

The Premier later estimated that a quarter of a million more would have left if there had

[15]Donald Lancaster, *The Emancipation of French Indochina* (London: Oxford University Press, 1961), p. 343.

35

been no harassments. "My own belief" wrote Dr. Tom Dooley, "is that this figure is not half large enough. The unbroken flow of the luckier, and of the wounded and mangled who made it to the American camps, was a clue to how many failed to make it." [16]

[16]Thomas A. Dooley, M.D., *Deliver Us From Evil* (New York: Farrar, Straus and Cudahy, 1956), p. 185.

CHAPTER FOUR
1954: DIEM IN POWER

1954: Diem in Power

When Ngo Dinh Diem returned to Vietnam in 1954 as Premier, he had a paper stating that he had full authority in both military and civil matters, and that South Vietnam was fully independent.

In reality, however, Diem had practically no powers. The military forces were controlled by a pro-French group, unfriendly to him and determined to replace him. The police power had been sold to a gang of ex-river pirates, whose principal income at the time came from the operation of vice dens in and around Saigon and Cholon. Control of the countryside was in the hands of various semi-religious groups and the Vietminh. The private sector of the Vietnamese economy was largely in the control of two groups of foreigners (French and Chinese) whose support of any Vietnamese regime would be half-hearted, to say the least. An agency of a foreign government controlled the financial and economic policy of Vietnam through its control of Vietnamese foreign exchange, and control of half the country was in process of being turned over to the Vietminh regime thanks to an international agreement which the South

Vietnamese representative at Geneva had quite properly refused to sign. "As it turned out, Diem possessed only a determination to make a reality out of the cruel mockery of the paper nominally giving him full powers."[1]

In July, 1954, there were in Britain, France, and the United States not half a dozen editorial writers, columnists, and foreign correspondents who believed that the anti-Communist government of South Vietnam, led by President Ngo Dinh Diem, could last. The overthrow of Diem's regime by the Communists was considered a certainty, and the fall of South Vietnam would greatly accelerate the Communist drive to conquer all of Southeast Asia, and would thus take on the proportions of a global disaster for the anti-Communist world.

Among those who at first shared this general pessimistic view of the prospects for South Vietnam was Joseph Buttinger of the International Rescue Committee in that country. Mr. Buttinger confessed:

> I went to Vietnam firmly convinced that the South could not survive, and in fact, I went chiefly because of this conviction. I wanted to see Saigon before it became a Communist city - something that I, like almost everyone whose judgment I valued, believed would happen in less than two years.[2]

By November 15, 1954, Buttinger became convinced that the Diem regime would not suc-

---

[1] Hoyt Price in Richard W. Lindholm, Ed., *Vietnam, The First Five Years* (Ann Arbor: Michigan State Press, 1959), p. 339.

[2] Joseph Buttinger, *The Smaller Dragon, A Political History of Vietnam* (New York: Praeger, 1958), p. 4.

cumb to the post-Geneva pressures of the Communists, internal and international; that he was a match for all French intrigues; that the armed politico-religious sects would have to submit to the national government or be defeated; and that the projected elections to "unify" North and South Vietnam would not be held, or if held, would certainly not produce a Communist majority in the South. And Communism, he was convinced, was not irresistible in Asia.

How did Buttinger come to change his mind? Because he and a minority of other thinking Americans in Saigon looked around and listened "more to the Vietnamese than to the French."[3] But most American correspondents, like Joseph Alsop (who wrote a series of defeatist articles in the *New York Herald Tribune* in December, 1954), went to Saigon merely looking for confirmation of their preconceptions about the futility of saving the country, and swallowed the French line.[4] Indeed the record of political reporting from South Vietnam, from Alsop in 1954 to David Halberstam in 1963, was a sorry one, and a poor reflection on American journalism. Most of these correspondents busied themselves with the task of undermining the Diem government, whether consciously or otherwise. The dissent of Buttinger, Marguerite Higgins and others was completely overshadowed by their defeatism.

Buttinger writes:
The two facts I learned and regarded as politically decisive were: (1) that the people were no longer interested in supporting the Communists, because they had sup-

[3]*Ibid.*, p. 5.
[4]*America,* January 29, 1955, p. 442.

ported them only to free themselves of the French more quickly; and (2) that South Vietnam had the leadership needed in her struggle to survive. I regarded Ngo Dinh Diem as a man of exceptional political talent, and expected his very shortcomings to turn into assets during the critical, early period of his regime.[5]

Similar sentiments were expressed by other qualified observers. Andre' Masson wrote: "The situation in the South, which seemed to most observers precarious in the extreme in 1954, was transformed very rapidly thanks to the energy and political sense of the person who took over the reins of government: Ngo Dinh Diem."[6] William Henderson asserted that "the survival of the Ngo Dinh Diem's ...government and the effective consolidation of its power throughout most of Free Vietnam in the first two years following the Geneva Agreement constitute a political miracle of the first magnitude."[7]

In September, 1954, the French-appointed chief of the army, General Nguyen Van Hinh, attempted to seize power, a move which was adroitly thwarted by Diem, who then fired him. Gradually, the Diem Government established full control over the army, but not without more French resistance and intrigue. Frightened by the Vietminh occupation of Hanoi, and convinced that Diem could not stave off the Communists alone, the French made a final effort to unseat him, in order to regain control of the South, and resume freedom of action in North

[5] Buttinger, *loc. cit.*
[6] *Histoire du Vietnam* (Paris: Presses Universitaires de France, 1960), p. 122.
[7] In Lindholm, *op. cit.,* p. 342.

Vietnam. "Ever since the military collapse of Tongking," according to the London *Economist* of January 8, 1955, "the French have in fact been ready to write off the Saigon government, and particularly since it has been led by a strong anti-French Prime Minister."

Meanwhile, the American decision to support Diem was strengthened by a report presented to the Senate's Foreign Relations Committee on October 15, which had been prepared by Senator Mike Mansfield after a two months' study tour through Indochina. Mansfield, after noting that Diem had "a reputation throughout Vietnam for intense nationalism and equally intense incorruptibility", stigmatized "the incredible campaign of subversion by intrigue", "the conspiracy of noncooperation and sabotage", which had hitherto prevented him from implementing "his constructive programme which consists of the elimination of some of the most brazen aspects of corruption and social inequity". In conclusion the Senator proposed that the policy of supporting Diem's Government, "based on the sound principles of national independence, an end to corruption and internal amelioration", should be pursued, while he recommended that in the event of a change of Government "the United States should consider an immediate suspension of all aid to Vietnam and French Union forces there, except that of a humanitarian nature, preliminary to a complete reappraisal of our present policies in Free Vietnam."[8]

On November 8, 1954, General Joseph Lawton Collins, President Eisenhower's special Am-

[8]U.S. Senate Foreign Relations Committee, *Report by Senator Mike Mansfield on a Study Mission to Vietnam, Cambodia, Laos* (Washington, October 1954).

bassador to South Vietnam, arrived in Saigon. This strengthened the position of Ngo Dinh Diem against the French. United States aid enabled the government to start a large-scale program of refugee resettlement. But the general conviction remained that South Vietnam could not hold out against Communist pressures from the North. Carl T. Rowan wrote that "The odds were considered at least eight to one against Diem and the free world."[9]

The first half of 1955 was a critical period for the Diem regime. United States support in these early days was invaluable. The U.S. agreed to channel aid directly to the Vietnamese, and not indirectly through the French, and a U.S. Army mission took over the training of the Vietnamese army from the French. Meantime, as the Diem government was increasingly threatened by troops of the Hoa Hao sect, it succeeded in taking away control of the Vietnamese armed forces from the French.

There is some question whether General Collins really thought that Diem was the best man to lead South Vietnam. According to Homer Bigart:

The Chief C.I.A. agent, Colonel Edward G. Lansdale, threw his support behind Ngo Dinh Diem, opposing the United States Ambassador, Gen. Lawton Collins, who recommended that the United States withhold support from the Saigon Government. Allen W. Dulles, then Director of the Intelligence Agency, persuaded his brother, Secretary of State, John Foster Dulles, that Colonel Lansdale was right.[10]

[9] *The Pitiful and the Proud,* New York, 1956, p. 350.
[10] *New York Times,* August 22, 1963.

In any event, the United States provided crucial support, including the extension of the protection of the South East Asia Treaty Organization to Free Vietnam, Cambodia, and Laos, by special protocol.[11] Meantime, with American aid, the Diem Government was accomplishing an almost impossible task in resettling the thousands of refugees from North Vietnam.

Yet it is extremely doubtful that without Diem, all the American aid in the world could have salvaged the situation. In the words of Ralph Lee Smith: "South Vietnam was fortunate in producing an able national leader at the time it won its independence. Confronted with almost insuperable difficulties, Diem played a totally unanticipated role of daring and sophistica-tion."[12] It soon became apparent that whereas Diem was still being berated by pro-French elements in Saigon, he was gaining in national stature among the common people. One ob-server had this to say about one of Diem's tours through the rice belt south of the 17th parallel in January, 1955: "Diem last week got his biggest ovation from his people. Rice growers thronged around him, beating gongs; soldiers competed to eat at his table; refugees chaired him around their hovels in informal marches of triumph," and concluded that this "confirmed that his strength lies increasingly among nationalist-minded villagers who suffered Communist depradations during the war, rather

[11]Russell H. Fifield, *The Diplomacy of Southeast Asia: 1945-1948* (New York: Harper, 1958), p. 317.

[12]"South Vietnam, A Success Story", *Foreign Policy Bulletin,* July 1, 1959.

than among the aperitif drinkers in French Saigon."[13]

According to Bernard Fall (who is very critical of Diem), the doughty Vietnamese patriot's "finest hour came, beyond a doubt, in the spring of 1955, when his chances of remaining in office seemed almost nil." Confronted with French intrigue and the revolt of the sects, "Diem, in addition to his qualities of personal courage and stubbornness, also displayed an uncanny ability to divide his enemies by a series of intricate maneuvers."[14] He also received wise counsel and support from members of his family: brothers Nhu, Archbishop Thuc, Can (later Governor of Central Vietnam), and Luyen (later Ambassador to Great Britain), together with Madam Nhu and nephew Tran Trung Dung.

In the early hours of March 29, 1955, Premier Diem was confronted with an ultimatum, a blunt threat to tear down the government of South Vietnam. The ultimatum came from the leaders of three religious-political sects of South Vietnam (Cao Dai, Hoa Hao, and Binh Xuyen),[15] "an exotic consortium of religious fanatics, feudal warlords, uniformed hoodlums and racket bosses bound loosely behind an

[13] *Time,* February 7, 1955.
[14] *The Two Vietnams,* p. 245.

[15]Two of the sects say they are religious; one is political. Cao Dai is a mixture of Christianity, Buddhism, Confucianism and Taoism with its own Pope and cardinals, and a Vatican headquarters 55 miles northwest of Saigon. Cao Dai has an expanding pantheon that includes Clemenceau, Victor Hugo and Joan of Arc and, in nomination pending his death, Sir Winston Churchill. Its Pope Pham Cong Tac was formerly a Saigon customs clerk. Hoa Hoa is a rowdy sect of dissindent Buddhists professing its belief in abstinence and prayer. Its founder, the late Huynh

ambitious general who keeps pet crocodiles".[16] Together the Sects had private armies numbering 40,000 men. Their leaders, having lost the French subsidies and prerogatives, were determined to exact comparable concessions from the new Vietnamese regime. "Reorganize your government within five days," said one of the sect spokesmen, and "Replace it with one that is suitable." Diem wanted to throw them out of his office, but his advisers, including Americans, urged him to go slowly. You are too weak to fight now, they counseled. Invite negotiations; play for time. Their advice was accepted. While soldiers and tanks moved through the tense streets of Saigon, the weanling government of South Vietnam dickered and maneuvered to avert civil war and whittle down the warlords of the sects.

The man who had to do the job was Premier Ngo Dinh Diem, "a resilient and deeply religious Vietnamese nationalist, burdened with the task of leading 10.5 million people of South Vietnam plus the continuing stream of refugees from the North from the brink of Communism to national independence and safety."[17] No man in troubled Asia was confronted with more obstacles on the road to order and justice. The sects, in control of a third of the southern half of the country in 1955, threatened not only his control, but

Phu So, augmented his fame as a healer when, the story goes, he was sent to a lunatic asylum and converted his psychiatrist. Binh Xuyen is an organization of bandits, in mustard-colored uniforms who controlled both the brothels and the police of Saigon under a handy arrangement with the absentee chief of state, Bao Dai. Their commander, General Le Van Vien, was once a river pirate.

[16] *Time,* April 4, 1955, p. 22.
[17] *Loc. Cit.*

also his life. The refugees, then in excess of 500,000 and coming into South Vietnam at the rate of 10,000 each week, were pleading for food, housing, and jobs.

Diem's refusal to comply with the ultimatum did not, however, lead to an outbreak of hostilities. The Hoa Hao, who controlled the ferries and river traffic in the delta, contented themselves with holding up food supplies for Saigon-Cholon, and the Binh Xuyen proceeded to entrench themselves in the police and security headquarters and in other requisitioned buildings in Saigon-Cholon. Diem then ordered paratroops under the command of Colonel Cao Van Tri to stand up to take over the police headquarters in the Boulevard Gallieni at the boundary of Saigon and Cholon and the security headquarters in Saigon. The occupation of police headquarters was carried out without difficulty, as the Binh Xuyen troops withdrew and established themselves in an adjacent building, but the Binh Xuyen commandos refused to evacuate the Security Service headquarters, and on the 28th the Prime Minister, whose readiness to accept a trial of strength was causing general dismay, ordered Colonel Tri to attack the building.[18] This attack was later countermanded at the instance of General Paul Ely, the French Commander-in-Chief, who objected to the operation on the grounds that French lives and property would be endangered. The outbreak of fighting had merely been postponed, however, until the night of the 29-30th when an affray took place around the police headquarters.

After the fighting, in which civilians were a target for both sides, had lasted for four hours,

[18] Pierre Dubard in *Figaro,* May 12, 1955.

the French Command was able to arrange for a cease-fire,[19] but this action was resented by Diem, who suspected the French of secretly supporting the sects, a suspicion apparently founded on a rumor that the Binh Xuyen had received French tactical advice during the fighting and on the fact that the French Command had refused to provide the national army with extra supplies of ammunition and fuel or with transport to move the parachute battalions from Nha Trang to Saigon.[20] General Lawton Collins, however, the American Ambassador Extraordinary, is reported to have approved Ely's action and to have betrayed increasing misgivings in regard to a policy directed to imposing upon the population of South Vietnam a Prime Minister whose leadership aroused such widespread opposition.[21]

These misgivings were shared by the bulk of Diem's supporters, who were nonplussed by his refusal to seek some compromise with the sects by which further bloodshed would be avoided. Their attitude was to have little effect upon the course of events since after the cease fire the direction of affairs was assumed by a junta comprising the Prime Minister, his brothers Ngo Dinh Nhu and Ngo Dinh Luyen, and their nephew by marriage, Tran Trung Dung.[22] This family junta was assisted by

[19]The casualties were army and police: 6 killed, 34 wounded; Binh Xuyen: 10 killed, 20 wounded; civilians: 10 killed, 58 wounded (Clos in *Le Monde,* Mar. 31, 1955).

[20]Clos in *Le Monde,* April 7, 1955.

[21]Dubard in *Figaro,* May 12, 1955.

[22]The junta's uncompromising approach to the situation was summed up on 6 April by an official spokesman in the following words: "We have the support of the entire population, who are imploring us to get rid of the Binh Xuyen bandits" (*Le, Monde,* April 7, 1955).

American advisers who were referred to enig-
matically by French press correspondents as
"the Americans who have an office in the Palais
Norodom",[23] or as the "young Colonels" attached to "certain American services".[24]

These Americans were Colonel Edward Lansdale, who with an assistant had been given office
accommodation at the palace, where their facilities for access to the Prime Minister were causing the French authorities some concern since
Lansdale was credited with pronounced "anti-
colonialist" views and with some important but
unspecified part in building up the authority
and popularity of the Filipino President, Ramon
Magsaysay.[25] Rumors were thus soon rife
that the advice which Lansdale was giving Diem
ran counter the American Ambassador's encouragement of Ely's efforts to prevent the outbreak
of civil war. But, if the American attitude appeared ambiguous, the French themselves were
believed to be in two minds about the situation.
This belief was based on reports that Commis-
sioner-General's staff was split into pro- and
anti-Diem factions, while the activities of certain
French officers gave rise to a suspicion that the
Expeditionary Corps was providing the sects
with unofficial support in their opposition to
the Prime Minister.[26]

With no personal political organization, a
civil service that was amateur and an army
still in training, Diem was charged with building a government and a popular base strong

[23] Dubard in *Figaro,* May 2, 1955.
[24] Guillain in *Le Monde,* May 18, 1955.
[25] Amoureux, *Croix sur l'Indochine* (1955), p. 90 and
Figaro, March 29, 1957.

[26] Lancaster, *op. cit.,* p. 387.

enough to overcome the strength and skill of Ho Chi Minh's Communist regime in North Vietnam. That he succeeded, represented an almost personal triumph for the Mandarin of Hue.

In a chapter entitled "The Miracle of Vietnam", Joseph Buttinger paid the following tribute to Ngo Dinh Diem: "His untainted integrity, his tenacious refusal to compromise with colonialism, and his profound insight into the political nature of his enemies were topped only by the courage he displayed toward friend and foe in creating the truly independent and strictly unified administration that his country then needed more than food and arms."[27] To this Buttinger added: "It is part of Ngo Dinh Diem's political greatness...to have understood that the sects, unhealthy product of the colonial past, could not be appeased but had to be destroyed."[28]

[27]In Lindholm, *op. cit.,* p. 30.
[28]*Loc. Cit.*

CHAPTER FIVE
1955: VICTORY, UNITY, CONSTITUTIONALISM

1955: Victory, Unity, Constitutionalism

Bao Dai ordered Ngo Dinh Diem to France on April 28, 1955, and appointed General Van Vy head of the national army, but Diem refused to comply with the order. He mobilized support for his government, and backed by a "Revolutionary Committee", resumed the struggle to oust the Binh Xuyen. The Revolutionary Committee demanded the ouster of Bao Dai as Chief of State, together with the withdrawal of all French troops. In May, the Government forces routed the Binh Xuyen, and gained control of the Saigon police, which had been under the Binh Xuyen up to that time. "Premier Diem, displaying the sort of strength that justified the high hopes many Americans had in him, moved with vigor against these unscrupulous river pirates".[1]

The total collapse of the religious sects' resistance against Ngo Dinh Diem sealed Bao-Dai's doom, although it is not quite accurate to say that he fully supported the sects against Ngo. In fact, according to Bernard Fall, the telegrams

[1]Army Vandenbosch and Richard A. Butwell, *Southeast Asia Among the World Powers* (Kentucky: University of Kentucky Press, 1957), p. 123.

exchanged between Bao Dai and Diem during that crucial period show that Diem requested Bao Dai's help in getting the three crack battalions of the Imperial Guard committed against the sects. Bao Dai consented, and in doing so, rejected the advice of his own close associates; he declared: "I do not wish it to be said later that, having to choose between his own selfish interests and the nation's survival, Bao Dai chose his own interests."[2] This action deprived Bao Dai of his last military leverage, and in fact ended any last lingering hopes of a political comeback.

Meantime, the French thought that Diem was now slipping out of their power, and that he was losing South Vietnam to the Communists in the process. But their efforts to salvage the situation for France were to no avail. The diplomatic and political infighting which accompanied the military operations of the Diem regime against the sects in the spring of 1955 remain unclear. Some claim that the French supported the sects against Diem, while others claim that certain key French units rendered assistance to the Vietnamese forces, thus paving the way for their victory over the sects.

On April 30, 1955, pro-Diem forces created a Revolutionary Committee, which convened a "General Assembly" of 200 delegates of eighteen political parties and groups. This Assembly voted a platform demanding the dismissal of Bao Dai, the formation of a new government under Ngo Dinh Diem, and the final and complete withdrawal of the French. Bao Dai's dethronement was announced on June 15, 1955,

---

[2] *The Two Viet-Nams,* p. 255.

and the way was open for the proclamation of the Vietnamese Republic.

The 1954 Geneva Agreement had called for an election in all Vietnam to establish a unified country. But the Government of South Vietnam had not signed the Geneva Agreement, because it considered partition and the other concessions to the Communists (including an International Control Commission in which India voted with Poland most of the time against Canada) as a betrayal. On July 16, 1955, Ngo Dinh Diem declared that South Vietnam, not being bound by the Geneva Agreement, would not take part in general elections unless they were guaranteed to be free in the North as well as in the South. When the Communist North refused to hold free elections, Diem proclaimed the Republic of Vietnam.

The State of Vietnam under Premier Diem took the position that the Saigon government was not technically bound by the cease-fire agreement; it stressed that the armistice was signed by a French officer of the French High Command. Nor did the State of Vietnam approve the "Final Declaration" of the Geneva Conference. Vietnamese Foreign Minister Tran Van Do, failing to obtain the intercession of the United States against the Anglo-French-Soviet accord on Vietnam, solemnly protested against "the hasty conclusion of the armistice agreement "between France and the Vietminh despite the control of Vietnamese troops by the French High Command "only through a delegation of authority by the Chief of State of Vietnam", against the abandoning of territory to the Vietminh, part of which was still in the possession of the State of Vietnam, and against "the fact that the French

High Command has arrogated to itself without preliminary agreement with the delegation of the State of Vietnam"[3] the right to fix the date of future elections, notwithstanding that a matter of a clearly political character was concerned. Opposed to the partition of his country, Tran Van Do subsequently resigned his post as Foreign Minister. In Saigon, Premier Diem in a broadcast on July 22, 1955 denounced the Geneva settlement and ordered flags at half mast for three days.[4]

On July 7, 1955 - the anniversary of the first year of the Diem regime - the Vietnamese Government announced that a national referendum would be held on October 23, to decide the issue between a monarchy vs. a republic. The result was a foregone conclusion: 98.2% in favor of a republic. Then on March 6, 1956, elections were held for a Constituent Assembly. Composed of 123 members spread over five political parties and a few independents, this Assembly was overwhelmingly pro-Diem.

Diem retained the theoretical "full civilian and military powers" granted him by Bao Dai until the proclamation of the Constitution of the Republic of Vietnam on October 26, 1956. At that date and until the expiration of his first Presidential mandate, on April 30, 1961, his full powers were reconfirmed by virtue of Article 98 of the Constitution, which provided that "during the first legislative term, the President of the Republic may decree a temporary suspension of virtually all civil rights to meet the legitimate demands of public security and order and of

[3]Protest by the Vietnamese Delegation, *Documents on American Foreign Relations,* 1954, p. 315.
[4]Fifield, *op. cit.,* p. 297.

national defense." But because of the continuing internal and external threat of the Vietcong, Diem's full powers were continued after that date. On October 18, 1961, the National Assembly proclaimed a state of emergency throughout Vietnam and voted Diem plenary powers for a period of one year, to be renewed if necessary. These powers were in fact renewed, until Diem was assassinated in November, 1963.

The South Vietnamese constitution was first drafted by an eleven-member Constitutional Commission which included well-known Vietnamese lawyers, aided by an American expert, Dr. J. A. C. Grant, and a Filipino lawyer, Juan C. Orendain. The document provides for a President without a Prime Minister, along American lines — a President imbued with as many powers, and perhaps even more, than the American President. Under Articles 44 and 98 of the Constitution, the President may proclaim a state of emergency or rule by decree, a provision reminiscent of the ill-famed Article 48 of the German Constitution under the Weimar Republic. Elected by universal suffrage on a joint ticket with his Vice-President for a five-year term, he is commander-in-chief of the armed forces, and like the American President has the power to appoint and dismiss senior civilian and military officers. He shares the treaty-making power with the legislature, and can call for a referendum with the consent of the Assembly.

The Constitution provides for separation of powers between the executive and legislative branches. The National Assembly is elected every four years. The judiciary is patterned on the French model, with a High Council of the Judiciary and a Constitutional Court; there is a liberal Bill of Rights, which, however, has been largely a dead letter because of the state of siege in which the country finds itself.

The National Assembly was criticized by enemies of the Diem regime as a rubber stamp affair, but even such anti-Diem writers as Bernard Fall admit that "some of the debates in 1956-1958 showed that there was a measure of lively opposition." But Fall, with his anti-Catholic bias, criticizes the ease with which the Diem regime passed "moral" legislation. I think it is fair to say that the Assembly was somewhere in between a completely free American Congress and a rubber-stamp totalitarian legislative body such as the Supreme Soviet. Proof that the Vietnamese National Assembly was no rubber stamp was evidenced, among other times, when a Bill for the Protection of Morality passed by only 68 votes out of 123. And even Fall admits that "the mere fact that the Assembly still attempts to criticize the executive branch does constitute a feeble sign of hope for the future of the country's institutions."[5] This was written before the much vaunted coup, which proceeded to abrogate the Constitution. But the critics of the old regime were curiously uncritical of the new one.

The highly-respected Leo Cherne described President Diem as "emphatic in his commitment to democratic ideals",[6] and the liberal Father Francis J. Corley asserted in 1961 that President Ngo Dinh Diem was "the dignified, but accountable magistrate of a free and great people."[7] On the other hand, there is no doubt

[5] *The Two Viet-Nams,* p. 268.
[6] *New York Times Magazine,* April 9, 1961.
[7] *Pacific Affairs,* July, 1961.

that not only was South Vietnam not ready for
democracy or able to adopt it, but that Ngo
Dinh Diem himself was less attracted to it than
he was to a vague mish-mash of ideas called
Personalism emanating from left-wing Catholic
circles in France, and especially the late Emman-
uel Mounier.   This seems to be a variety of
humanism and "social Catholicism", where the
emphasis is less on democracy than it is on
"good" (albeit authoritarian) government.   One
American expert who spent eighteen months in
Saigon trying to reform South Vietnam's taxa-
tion system defined Personalism as a "confused
melange of papal encyclicals and kindergarten
economics...(combined with) a suspicion of private businessmen, a fear of foreign capital, and
an attitude that little can be accomplished in
Vietnam without direct government ownership
and control."[8]   There has been much criticism
of strong-arm methods and government by family, but this is not peculiar to South Vietnam.
Professor Wesley Fishel wrote that the "relaxed
relationship" between the Saigon police and the
citizens "suggests that accusations of authori-
tarianism lack solid substance."[9]   But the Diem
Government could hardly relax given the nature
of the internal and external threat.   Without
the Communist threat, it might have been possible to realize many of the freedoms in South
Vietnam that we have in the United States.   Yet
even there the remnants of the sects and French-
engendered jealousies were waiting to take advantage of Diem's weakness; so were anti-Diem
Americans stationed in Saigon.

[8]Milton C. Taylor, "South Vietnam: Lavish Aid,
Limited Progress," *Pacific Affairs,* Fall, 1961, p. 252.
[9]*Problems of Freedom,* p. 25.

I remember very well my visit to that city in 1958. A senior Foreign Service Officer went to great lengths to discredit the Diem regime, magnify its shortcomings, ridicule Diem's religion and his family, and to urge for a change in U.S. policy. He did this openly to a visiting group from The National War College, Washington, D.C. Almost from the very start, certain American government officials and newsmen were anxious to find fault with Diem and his government, giving little thought to what might come next. The minor paratroop putsch of November 11, 1960 apparently had the approval and perhaps also some encouragement from some Americans in Saigon.[10] Even the liberal *New York Times* expressed pleasure that "President Ngo Dinh Diem has survived this major test of his power."[11]

Most American observers conceded that while Diem, for many complex reasons (among them, no doubt, his mandarin heritage and the spiritual detachment natural to a devout Catholic in a country where Catholics were a minority), did not measure up to Western ideals of democracy, he did appear "honestly to want to introduce democracy."[12] The big question was when and how. Diem contended that it had to be introduced "from the bottom up," and to this end he instituted the "strategic hamlet" program, under which half of Vietnam's sixteen thousand villages were gradually made capable of resisting attack by the Vietcong terrorists. Villages that have reached strategic status are visited

[10]Renee Grosset, "Les ennuis du President Diem", *Le Figaro,* November 21, 1960.
[11]*New York Times,* November 13, 1960.
[12]Shaplen, *op. cit.,* p. 125.

by civic-action teams, trained to strengthen the bonds between the villagers and their government, help them build schools and hospitals, to form agricultural cooperatives, to establish freely elected local councils, and initially to select the leaders who will launch the local councils.

Some Americans complained about the slowness with which local democracy developed, and charged that the "strategic hamlet" concept had failed. They have noted President Diem's stubbornness, and his unwillingness to take advice from Americans. Obdurate and imperious as Diem seemed to many Americans, no fair appraisal of the man can fail to take into consideration his mandarinic training and principled purpose, his patience, loyalty to clan, and courage. "Nor should it be forgotten that he proved himself to be the right man in the right place at the right time when, almost alone during the year or so after the French debacle, he rode out the storm of anarchy that very nearly swamped the new Republic of Vietnam." [13]

At a meeting of American Friends of Vietnam in 1956, General John W. O'Daniel (and others, including Senator John F. Kennedy) paid tribute to President Diem and his cause. O'Daniel listed Diem's accomplishments up to that time as: successful movement and resettlement of the refugees; reorganization of the army into an efficient team loyal to the government and capable of defending the country; victory over the sects. "President Diem told me on my departure that he has been called a dictator," said General O'Daniel. "The war is on," Diem told him, "and I must use warlike methods. I have to retain

[13] *Ibid.*, pp. 128, 131.

close control of my Cabinet and people until we win the war against Communist infiltration."[14]

At the same meeting former Under Secretary of State, Walter S. Robertson, praised the "dedication, courage and resourcefulness of President Diem....In him, his country has found a truly worthy leader whose integrity and devotion to his country's welfare have become generally recognized among his people. Asia has given us in President Diem another great figure, and the entire free world has become the richer for his example of determination and moral fortitude."[15]

In 1959 R. G. Casey, Australian Minister for External Relations, wrote that it is unfair to judge Vietnam by American standards.

Two facts should be remembered in any criticism of Vietnam's administration. First, Vietnam is in the front line of the cold war....Its government cannot afford to leave openings which its opponents could exploit. This would be fatal not only to Vietnam, but most detrimental to the interests of freedom in southeast Asia. Second, the exercise of democracy on a national scale is a totally new concept in Vietnam and, it will take time for institutions, traditions, and habits to be developed which will enable democratic rights to be exercised in a constructive and responsible way. Political consciousness in a people is not necessarily a slow growth, but it has to grow deep as well as wide if it is to be sound. Even the concept of loyalty to the state and to their govern-

[14]American Friends of Vietnam, *America's Stake in Vietnam* (New York: Carnegie Press 1956), p. 96.
[15]*Ibid.,* p. 15.

ment is a novel one to the Vietnamese. Only the Vietnamese can work out their political development.[16]

Another close observer of developments in Vietnam, raised the question:

But if Diem will not change—and a good many dedicated Americans have tried to make him change—should the United States simply withdraw its support and accept chaos? It is not good enough in this unhappy day and age simply to dismiss a man such as Diem as an utter impossibility, a contradiction in terms, in a country 90% illiterate....Diem has created strength miraculously, in a vacuum of despair. That he has done so through excessive repression is regrettable, but relatively irrelevant.[17]

[16]In Lindholm, *op. cit.,* p. 344.
[17]John M. Mecklin, *ibid.,* pp. 354, 355, 358.

CHAPTER SIX

1956-1961: ECONOMICS
AND POLITICAL EVOLUTION

1956-1961: Economic and
Political Evolution

In October, 1955, Diem issued a decree which aimed at breaking up the large landholdings created during the colonial period. While genuine land reform was going on in South Vietnam, things were quite different in the North. According to Ellen Hammer, "The northern agrarian reform program degenerated into an instrument of terror devoid of any economic justification and the indiscriminate purge directed against groups of people who by no definition could legitimately be regarded as big landowners, had such a demoralizing effect on the population that sporadic risings broke out in November, 1956 north of the seventeenth parallel; and the D. R. V. N. (Democratic Republic of Viet-Nam) finally had to admit publicly the breakdown of its agrarian reform program."[1]

During this period vast programs were undertaken to resettle the refugees. As soon as portions of the countryside were made secure from rebel armed forces, land reform was instituted, and tracts of several acres were made available to the refugees, along with necessary imple-

[1]"Progress Report on Southern Viet Nam", *Pacific Affairs,* Vol. XXX, No. 3, September, 1957.

ments, supplies, and credits to begin their new life.

The Ministry of Land Development transferred thousands of families from the overcrowded coastal areas to the sparsely inhabited uplands in the central part of the country. An example is the area nearby Banmethout: in late 1958 there was nothing except tropical jungle; but by late 1960 there was a new agricultural village, with 1400 people living in neat thatch-roofed cottages, growing coffee, peanuts, cassava (for tapioca), sugar cane, and other commercial crops. By April, 1960, 120 such villages had been established, and nearly 200,000 people relocated.[2]

Vietnam's land reform program was modeled to some extent on the programs which had been carried out after World War II in Japan and Taiwan. Wolf Ladejinsky, who had played a prominent role in the Japan and Taiwan planning, became Diem's chief economic adviser for land reform in Vietnam. All holdings in excess of 245 acres were surrendered to the government for redistribution to the tenants or landless cultivators. Landowners are reimbursed, receiving ten percent of the value of their land in cash, and the rest in bonds which can be used to buy shares in government-owned industries or to pay taxes. In this way, land reform and reinvestment in industry are accomplished simultaneously. The program will ultimately result in the resettlement of about three million Vietnamese on land which they will own.

When the fertile Mekong River delta was wrested from Hoa Hao troops, a great redevel-

[2]Benjamin L. Masse, "The Revolt in Vietnam," *America,* November 26, 1960, p. 301.

opment project was started. Known as the Cai-san project, it involved the opening of old canals, the digging of new ones, and the settlement of refugees on 7.5 acre tracts. By 1957 enough rice was being grown in the Mekong delta to supply Vietnam's own population and to provide a substantial surplus for export.

The army was reorganized and trained under United States guidance, and reduced to half its former size. American aid was indispensable to the country's survival and, on the whole, was planned and administered with considerable skill and success. In 1957, United States aid paid for half the government budget, including the full payroll of the armed forces, and covered nearly three-fourths of the nation's imports.

With the opening of the rice fields and the return of the country to a self-sustaining agricultural economy, an increasing measure of stability was attained. As early as 1957 the government began to study the problems which will be its major concern during the years immediately ahead. Vietnam's resources are primarily agricultural. Few areas in Asia have such a favorable ratio of land to population. Before the war, Vietnam exported rice and rubber in an intensive two-crop economy. France underwrote its foreign trade deficit.

The rebuilding of these two crops for export is a keystone in the Government's current efforts to pay its own way in world trade. Both the strength and vulnerability of such an economy have been demonstrated within the past two years. In 1957 exports of both crops were sizable but in 1958 a poor crop and the world recession created serious difficulties.

While these two products have been intensively cultivated, Vietnam has found it necessary to import many agricultural commodities which might well be grown at home. One phase of the government's attack on its trade deficit, therefore, has been concerned with broadening the base of domestic agricultural production.

North of the Mekong delta are a series of uplands and plateaus which had not previously been cultivated. Through ancient custom, Vietnamese farmers have confined themselves to raising rice in the lowlands. In 1956 a United Nations survey team confirmed the potential capacity of these uplands to provide a more diversified agriculture.

The government has embarked on a large-scale resettlement program aimed at producing a broad variety of food staples in the rich plateau areas. This program requires the introduction of new crops, the development of new skills, and the breaking of centuries-old customs. The success of these efforts will have an important effect on Vietnam's balance of trade and on the problems created by an agricultural system based on a single food crop.

Another major factor in Vietnam's foreign trade, as well as in its domestic economy, has been its almost complete lack of manufacturing facilities. The country lacks the resources for heavy industry, but offers many opportunities for the development of lighter manufacturing enterprises based on readily available raw materials.

Power is a major problem. Vietnam has one coal mine, no oil as far as anyone knows, and a hydroelectric potential which is promising but would require vast sums of capital to develop.

A start has been made, however, in the development of certain light industries. Intensive efforts are being deployed to attract foreign capital, and in some instances these efforts have been successful: the building of a textile mill, a sugar mill, a glass factory, a fish processing plant, and a pharmaceutical factory. Factories for producing paper and building board from Vietnam's rich forest resources were recommended by the UN survey team, and are being eagerly sought by the government.

Future development will depend in considerable measure on Vietnam's success in attracting capital on a scale sufficient to develop an adequate basis for domestic production. The government has passed many laws providing for investment opportunities, either wholly developed by foreign capital or developed by foreign capital in conjunction with government investment. It is, of course, true that private capital in the wealthier nations of the West can usually find investment opportunities at home. Moreover, the creation of the industries which would be most desirable in a balanced development plan does not always bring a rapid return on investment. The next four or five years will show whether Vietnam can fulfill its ambitious hopes for investment of foreign capital in its economy.

Despite its vulnerability to world prices and conditions, Vietnam must make intensive efforts in the next few years to increase substantially exports of its two basic crops - rice and rubber. This is particularly true for the immediate future, when United States aid will diminish and Vietnam will have few other products it can sell to compensate for the resulting decline in revenues.[3]

In March, 1957, the government of President Ngo Dinh Diem announced a series of regulations intended to encourage foreign investments. Thus up to this time, real progress was being made on all fronts except the political front. But the Diem government argued plausibly that democracy on a national scale would have to await better understanding of this term by the people, a higher level of education, and, most importantly an end to the internal and external threat to the very existence of the infant republic.

President Diem and the members of his government were deeply preoccupied by the need for a unified cultural and intellectual alternative to the challenge of communism, and were convinced that the country's survival depended on its success in formulating such an alternative. Diem himself subscribed to a philosophy which he termed "personalism," and which involves strong emphasis on the development of the individual as the end and justification of government.

According to Henry G. Fairbanks: "The Communists fear this ideology more than they fear his 170,000 man, American-trained army. Diem's vision is not enervated by the skepticism of a Nehru. It is not sapped by the shifty opportunism of a Sukarno. It is, in its very over-simplifications, the sole positive response to come out of non-Communist Asia which can meet the Communist challenge on equal terms - of definiteness and dream....But it is doubtful if many American economic advisers grasp its

[3]Ralph Lee Smith, "South Vietnam, A Success Story," *Foreign Policy Bulletin,* July 1, 1959.

import.   Thinking in terms of other imports, strong on statistics but weak in philosophy, knowing more of world markets than of human motivations, they dismiss or deride Diem's Personalism." Fairbanks went on to say of Diem: "...the massive dedication of the man is unmistakable.   In a world floundering to define national goals, this rare man gives the impression that he knows where he is going. And something in his steady movement carries others along, if only partly or uncomprehendingly."[4]

The military coup in Laos on August 9, 1960, which replaced a pro-Western government with a neutralist regime, had important repercussions in Vietnam. Now the Communists, supported by the Soviet Union, could openly cross over from Laos into South Vietnam, vastly complicating the defense problems of President Diem.

Then, on November 11, 1960, there was an attempted coup in Saigon. Paratroop battalions led by Col. Nguyen Van Thy and Lt. Col. Vuong Van Dong tried to overthrow President Diem, and attacked the Presidential palace. But loyal troops repelled the attack, and the threat was overcome.

The rapid and dangerous spread of Communist terrorism and sabotage in South Vietnam during the early months of 1961 caused increasing concern among the Western powers, and British Foreign Secretary Lord Home (returning to London from a SEATO Council meeting in Bangkok) declared on March 30, 1961 that there was "a very real danger" of a Communist take-over in South Vietnam. On May 4, 1961

[4]"The Enigma of Ngo Dinh Diem", *The Commonweal*, September 21, 1962, pp. 516, 517.

U.S. Secretary of State Dean Rusk declared at his press conference that South Vietnam would receive added assistance from the U.S., both military and economic, and that a situation like that in South Vietnam "cannot be dealt with solely in military terms." Rusk directly accused the Communist Party of North Vietnam for the upsurge of Communist guerrilla activity in South Vietnam, and he declared that the North Vietnamese Communist Party at its Third Congress on September 10, 1960 "adopted a resolution which declared that the Vietnamese revolution has as a major strategic task the liberation of the South from the 'rule of United States imperialists and their henchmen.' This resolution called for the direct overthrow of the Government of the Republic of Vietnam."

On October 2, 1961, President Ngo Dinh Diem declared in the National Assembly: "It is no longer a guerrilla war we have to face but a real war waged by an enemy who attacks us with regular units fully and heavily equipped and who seeks a strategic decision in Southeast Asia in conformity with the orders of the Communist International." A few days after this pessimistic statement, President Kennedy announced that he was sending his chief military adviser, General Maxwell D. Taylor, to investigate the military situation in South Vietnam, so that the U.S. could undertake measures to prevent South Vietnam from falling to the Communists.

South Vietnam's position was seriously weakened early in 1961 when the United States decided to end its support of the anti-Communist forces in Laos, and accept a coalition government in Vietnam, in which the Communists and neutralists held the upper hand. General Lyman Lemnitzer, Chairman of the Joint Chiefs of Staff, went so far as to say: "The United States has lost the battle of Laos." President Diem was bitter at U.S. vacillation on Laos, and one of his aides predicted: "The U.S. will now wait until China has the A bomb and then cry 'we cannot act now because the Chinese will bomb Saigon, Tokyo, and Taipan. "[5]

Vice President Lyndon B. Johnson was sent to south-east Asia and particularly to Saigon to spread comfort. When he arrived in Vietnam, he expected to find Diem jittery over the loss of Laos. Instead, Diem censured the U.S. for "letting down" its allies in Loas. Johnson described Diem as the "Winston Churchill of Asia," and praised his resettlement of refugees, the development of roads and railroads, and the growing agricultural output.[6]

Early in 1961, the Diem regime enacted certain reforms, designed to meet Vietnamese and American criticism. These provided for more self-government in the villages, and administrative reforms in Saigon. *The New York Times* praised these reforms in an editorial (June 13, 1961) and declared that "President Ngo Dinh Diem has reorganized his Government, concentrating executive authority in three strong ministries....these changes promise better operating efficiency."

Presidential elections were held in 1961. Among the opposition candidates were Nguyen Thanh Quat, a wealthy forty-four year old plantation owner and Nguyen The Truyen, with a long record of anti-French nationalism. Tru-

[5] *Newsweek,* May 22, 1961, pp. 35, 36.
[6] *Loc. Cit.*

yen's campaign manager was Nhiem Xuan Thien, publisher of the newspaper *Thoi-Luan*, which had been banned earlier by the Government. For a country like Vietnam, these elections were certainly a step in the direction of democracy, and even the critical Fall admits that the opposition "managed to get some of its case to the public in Saigon, where foreign journalists could watch the proceedings."[7] *Time* reported that the "much-abused Diem had run a reasonably honest election--and won", while the *New York Times* explained the heavy pro-Diem vote (88%) as due to the country's "considerable prosperity." The *Times* declared that it had been a "double victory" over the Communist and non-Communist opposition, due mostly to the "reform programs;" it asserted that the over-all results had been a "crushing repudiation of Communism as well as a public tribute to the strong-willed leader."[8] But the opposition remained and as in most underdeveloped countries, it relied on force to achieve its ends. Meantime, the United States Government, in its tradition of idealism, kept pressing the Diem regime for more reforms. American policy-makers could not seem to understand that an imperfect regime was better than one operated by the Vietcong.

Possibly the fiasco in Laos had something to do with bringing the "reform-at-any price" idealists of the State Department to heel. In February, 1962, the United States blocked all further aid to the anti-Communist Laotian regime of General Phoumi Nosavan, which finally forced him into a disastrous coalition regime with the Communists and neutralists. As more

[7] *The Two Viet-Nams,* p. 276.
[8] *New York Times,* April 10, 1961.

Laotian territory came under the control of the Communist-neutralist coalition, and as public fears in Vietnam were voiced that a similar policy was being "actively considered" for Vietnam, there occurred a modification of U.S. policy. It was decided to make the defeat of the Vietcong come first, reforms later. Meantime, the Diem Government adopted a reform program inspired by a mission to Vietnam headed by Dr. Eugene Staley. This included, among other items, improved training for local officials to improve their rapport with the people, and an aid program to improve the lot of the loyal mountaineer minorities.

On February 15, 1962, U.S. Ambassador Frederick Nolting told the Saigon Rotary Club that the "Vietnamese Government, under the devoted and courageous leadership of Ngo Dinh Diem, attempts to realize, under difficult conditions, political, social, and economic progress for the people, with the help of the United States." Acknowledging that "some among you found that the advantages of a free society were not coming down to the people," Ambassador Nolting emphasized that the United States was giving its fullest support to the "elected and constitutional regime." He added: "What a marvelous transformation would take place in this country if all those who criticize their government would decide to work with it and for it."[9]

But some of the anti-Diem newsmen in Saigon would not be placated. Their criticism of Diem far exceeded any harsh words for Ho Chi Minh. At a time of "managed news" in Washington, they accused the Vietnamese Government of following the same tactics.

[9]*Agence France-Presse,* February 16, 1962.

Because U.S. officials and newsmen continued to publicly suggest that Diem was expendable, the President began to tighten up security, and called some units in from the front to safeguard the position of the government in Saigon. Early in March, 1962, the Presidential palace was strafed by two dissident pilots, in what was termed an "isolated" attack. According to one reporter, "The President himself came through the assassination attempt with courage and coolness."[10] Within two hours he was on the radio with a brief recorded speech to thank "divine protection" for his escape. Then he paid a hospital visit to the soldiers wounded in the attack, and re-assured the mutinous pilots' fellow officers that they would bear no share of the blame.

President Kennedy immediately sent a message that denounced the attack as a "destructive and vicious act," and expressed relief that Diem was "safe and unharmed." The quick U.S. reaction was "intended to show that any hidden sympathizers of the mutinous pilots could expect no backing from Washington."[11]

On October 6, 1962, the *New York Times* editorialized that the "news from South Vietnam recently has been encouraging," and credited this improvement to such "administrative improvements" as the construction of strategic hamlets and better relations with anti-Communist mountaineers. Joseph Alsop and other objective reporters also contradicted some of the more hysterical anti-Diem newsmen, such as Homer Bigart, Francois Sully, and David Halberstam. (Alsop, originally anti-Diem, changed his views).

[10] *Time,* March 9, 1962, p. 29.
[11] *Loc. cit.*

At the end of December, 1962, the Diem Government announced that 4,077 (out of a projected 11,182) strategic hamlets had been completed, and that 39% of South Vietnam's population was living in these communities. According to the *New York Times*:

> The greatest advance in the hamlets has been psychological...for the erection of barbed wire and bamboo fences has given a sense of unity and identity to the peasants. Establishment of hamlet councils has linked many of these communities to the national Government for the first time. Where three or four armed Viet Cong troopers could formerly enter a hamlet, recruit a few youngsters and terrorize one or two residents, they now have to attack the whole community.... The guerrillas have grown wary of making frontal assaults in some areas because of increased resistance by hamlet guards armed by the Government with carbines, shotguns and grenades. Another factor contributing to improvement of hamlet defense has been the establishment of 1,500 radio transmitters in villages (collections of hamlets comparable to counties in the United States.) These transmitters permit residents to call immediately for military help. The security of the strategic hamlets has encouraged the Government to reinstate a program of credits to farmers. Formerly, Viet Cong terrorists squelched menaced farmers who accepted Government loans or tried to pay them back. [12]

[12]Paris edition, December 15, 1963.

CHAPTER SEVEN

DIEM SPEAKS

Diem Speaks

When he was asked to explain the role of Free Vietnamese to an Australian journalist when he visited Sydney in 1957, President Ngo-Dinh Diem engaged in no hyperbole. He went straight to the point when he declared:

> By its geographical situation Viet Nam occupies a key position on the classical road of invasion of South-East Asia. Whether one likes it or not, the existence of a free and independent Viet Nam is a guarantee of the independence and freedom of the non-Communist nations of Asia.

Asked what progress Viet Nam had achieved since arriving at independence, President Diem said:

> The Asian masses are very impatient to catch up with the West, but newly-independent countries encounter many handicaps. They are short of executive personnel. War has caused widespread destruction. In our country, less than two years ago, political parties, each with its private army, each in the hope of personal profit, were fighting one another to seize power. All these might be termed the classical phenomena of anarchy which generally follow upon the period of accession to independ-

ence.   The Asian countries, therefore, do not enjoy the ideal conditions to meet the impatience of the masses, if ordinary methods are used.

In our efforts to reconstruct Viet Nam we chose a line of action conforming to historical facts, taking into account the psychological and material conditions which I have just outlined.

We first of all gained control of a chaotic situation seemingly past mending. We recovered command of our police and army which had been in foreign hands. We reorganized the administration which had formerly been powerless to cope with the feudal sects.   By these means we regained and maintained that internal security indispensable to organising constitutional legislative elections to provide the country with a Republican Constitution and a National Assembly.

We have resettled more than 800,000 refugees, representing over one-tenth of the population, upon fertile lands which had formerly been the exclusive preserve of the feudal elements, and of the Communists. We have above all restored confidence among our people, and stability in political life.   These are the two essential conditions of the economic reconstruction of our country.

In this field also, together with the programme of industrialisation of our country our aim is to provide each family with a basic small property.   To that end we are accelerating the settlement of landless people on hitherto unused fertile lands, particularly in the High Plateaux. At the same time, and in order to increase the basic elementary prosperity of our country we are introducing community development in the villages involving large schemes at village level. Roads, dykes, pumping stations are being built by the village people with the aid of Government technical experts.

Surprising results have been attained in the space of a few months, both psychologically and materially.

With political stability restored and the essential needs of the people met, we hope to take another big step in the general reconstruction of the country.

When he was asked what in his opinion was the role of Viet Nam and Malaya as independent leaders in South-East Asia, President Diem replied:

As far as Viet Nam is concerned we entertain no ambition of being the leader of anyone. We seek to solve our own problems as best we can.

It is true that our problems are the same as those of other Asian countries. The intellectual rigorousness with which we have conducted our internal affairs and the sincerity of our peaceful intentions have gained for our country the sympathy of the leaders of Asia. In that respect we are very honoured.

When President Diem visited Korea in 1957 he addressed the National Assembly of Korea at Seoul when he made a number of pointed references to the horrors created by Communism.

Said the President:

What makes the destiny of Asia so tragic, when she has just freed herself from oppression and is hardly ready to deal with the difficult problems arising out of the post-colonial state of anarchy, is the necessity for her to fight anew another system of oppression, so much more serious and dangerous - the Communist system.

In a climate laden with threats of war externally and with revolutionary tension internally, it placed in question the hard-won independence and liberty.

To the considerable material difficulties of such a situation are added the intellectual apprehension and the moral disarray resulting from the discrepancy between the vision of reconquered independence leading without delay to freedom and economic progress, and the stern reality of the strict discipline of community action demanded by modern technology and the struggle against Communism.

The hard necessity of fighting again after so much hope and after long years of toiling, suffering and sacrifice, is a cause of disappointment in some, of the discouragement of others, but for still others it has led to the search for a way of escape from concrete and historical realities.

Yet, no shirking of responsibility, directly or indirectly, could free us from a tragic reality, which is our present destiny.

If we do not wish to betray all those who have given their lives for our common cause we must face that destiny with courage and with the means which are historically within our reach.

This is precisely what the Korean and Vietnamese people have done.

As their ancestors had reacted in the great crisis of our national history, the Vietnamese people have stood up against the tremendous material and political difficulties which assailed Viet Nam after Geneva had plunged even the best of her sons into a state of apprehension coloured by despair.

It has drawn the necessary strength for the retrieving of a seemingly desperate situation from a spontaneous return to its great traditions of political unity and respect for the human being.

It is this fundamental urge to base action on definite and concrete cultural traditions which have given Viet Nam's political life its special character, clarity and forcefulness.

It is by being faithful to these traditions that the Vietnamese people have subdued quickly and with determination this postcolonial anarchy which dislocated the country and rendered it impotent to accomplish the tasks of political and economic reconstruction.

The suppression of the large armed bands has made possible the organisation of a referendum for the establishment of the Republic, and of constitutional and legislative elections which have given the country both a Constitution and our National Assembly.

The principles which guided us in drawing up our Constitution are respect for the human being, endowed with freedom and a sense of responsibility both in his inner and community life, as well as in his relationship to God.

Making the human being the source of freedom and of creation, the very core of our political, economic, social and cultural structure, the Republic of Viet Nam accepts from its inception the evolution and the broadening of the regime toward an ever greater democratic progress, to responsibility, and to spiritual life.

However, the most lofty principles are useless without men. Only men can mature and implement these principles. That is why the Government of Viet Nam believes that in addition to the idea of the free development of his intellectual, moral and spiritual life must be encouraged. We believe that we are justified in protecting these fundamental rights.

In doing this we pursue two aims.

First we want to re-arm the Vietnamese citizen morally and to make him impervious to all tyranny, whatever its origin.

Second, we want to reinforce the spiritual cohesion of the Vietnamese peoples - cohesion which accounts for the capacity to enjoy for many centuries a largely decentralised system without falling into anarchy. Yet this cohesion has been largely shaken by the impact of the West.

Yet man does not live only by the idea of liberty. He must be given a minimum of material support which will guarantee that liberty. That is the aim of our land reform and especially of the effort to develop the large but hitherto undeveloped regions of the country. This policy will provide each landless family with a little house and enough land for its maintenance.

To ensure the well-being of the people the Government is ready to assist them in other directions which make it possible for a healthy and prosperous country. This objective is being sought through community development work by which the village people execute, with the technical aid of the Government, big schemes on a communal basis.

In a speech made at the State dinner given in his honor by President Syngman Rhee of Korea, President Ngo-Dinh Diem further enlarged on this theme.

He said:

With the Korean people, the peoples of Viet Nam have accepted very heavy sacrifices in order to defend not only their territory, but also the liberty and the independence of more privileged countries situated outside the friction zone of the two worlds.

Both Korea and Viet Nam have had, in the course of their long histories, to struggle incessantly in order to preserve their existence and the national character.

That common struggle has continued since our two countries were cut in two by Communism.

From this day one identical aim must guide our efforts — the reunification of our territories for the liberation of our peoples from foreign Communist domination.

When he delivered an address at Seoul University where he was invested with the degree of Doctor of Law, President Ngo-Dinh Diem returned once again to attack. He said:

At a time when Marxist science is but a passing manifestation in European thought, Communism, by flood and fire, seeks to impose its political domination and its universal tyranny of the mind upon Asia. It is comforting to see the Korean intellectual elite take up the challenge and united in defending Asian culture.

Twice in the space of a century Asia has been shaken by the materialistic aggressiveness of the West — the first time with the Opium War, and the second time with the unleashing of fanaticism and Communist intolerance which we are witnessing today.

The works of the Asian intellectuals teach us that behind the massive character of the technique by which the West has dominated us, we must seek to grasp the spirit which engenders that technique and to understand that this spirit, born of Grecian logic and of the evangelical message, is of a true and permanent value to civilisation.

But, the technique presented by Communism is bereft of that spirit. Technical progress, and the development of teaching in the Communist countries aim uniquely at industrialisation and propaganda. The persecution of academic people which is raging in the lands of the hundred flowers exposes the fundamental lack of culture and the systematic ignorance of the Communist leaders of all that lies outside Marxism.

In fact, in these countries, national cultures are relegated to the domain of folklore.

Nevertheless, we must not forget that the technical effectiveness represented by Communist enterprises exercises a great temptation to the Asian masses who are impatient to eradicate their technical backwardness and are thirsty for social justice.

It is, therefore, necessary for Asian intellectuals to go back to the authentic sources of Asian thought, and at the same time to draw inspiration from the permanent values of Western culture with a view to indicating to statesmen the guiding principles which should motivate them in solving the great problems of Asia without losing Asia's spiritual origins.

It is necessary to disengage Asian philosophical thought from the verbal lyricism which disperses its subject to the point where the ego is suppressed, and from the narrow moulds which imprison and sterilise it. [1]

[1]Sirdar Ikbal Ali Shah, *Vietnam* (London: Octagon Press, 1960), pp. 109-114.

CHAPTER EIGHT

1962-1963: INTRIGUES AND
THE "BUDDHIST" CRISIS

1962-1963: Intrigues and the "Buddhist" Crisis

One of the reasons that the United States lost out in Laos in 1961 was the victory of the State Department "doves" over the Central Intelligence Agency "hawks." The hawks had supported anti-Communist General Phoumi Nosavan against the Communist neutralist coalition (princes Souvannavong and Souvanna Phouma), whereas the doves favored a coalition of all three factions in preference to the "risky" strategy of supporting the anti-Communists, With the advent of the Kennedy Administration the doves won out, and U.S. forces withdrew from Laos, and cut off all aid to the anti-Communists.

Early in 1963, the same sort of struggle was going on inside the U.S. Government. The C.I.A. man in Saigon, John Richardson, had close and friendly ties with the Diem regime; he, U. S. General Paul Harkins, and Ambassador Nolting all favored support of the admittedly imperfect Diem regime against the real threat, which was Communism. But in Washington, certain elements in the State Department and Executive Office of the White House favored a policy of disengagement from Diem, while casting about for some "third force". This group, headed by Assistant Secretary of State, Roger Hilsman and Averill Harriman, encouraged by leftist journalists in Saigon, began to undermine the positions of Diem, Harkins, and Nolting. Hilsman and Harriman had been part of the "dove" contigent in Laos. President Kennedy began to listen to them more and more, while downgrading the view of the Defense Department and the C.I.A.

In Saigon itself, there were some Foreign Service Officers who collaborated in this venture, against their field boss, Ambassador Nolting. One of these was Charge d'Affaires William Truehart. On June 11, 1963, while President Diem was in Saigon Cathedral attending a Mass for Pope John XXIII, Truehart told a press conference that the United States would "disassociate" itself from Diem's policies and publicly condemn him. The battle was on to dump Nolting, Richardson and General Harkins, and it was two-thirds won when the anti-Diem generals were incited to violence on November 1st.

Meantime correspondents who had maintained a remarkable "objectivity" about Communist dictators stepped up their campaign of vilification and abuse against Ngo Dinh Diem and his family. Just as Herbert Matthews had been a partisan of the Spanish "Loyalists" and of Castro, with no pretense at objective news reporting, so did David Halberstam openly espouse the cause of an agglomeration of anti-Diem elements, going out of his way to magnify shortcomings, true and imagined, of the Diem entourage. The opposition was always "democratic" and "progressive." An example of the extreme to which the anti-Diem clique went is an article by Stanley Karnow *(Saturday Evening Post,* September 28, 1963), in which he attacked all the Ngos, including Ngo Dinh Can, "who cared for the brothers' aging mother (past 80, she is bed-ridden and silently lies in state, like a wax mummy, occasionally visited by dutiful officials)."

The "Buddhist crisis" in the spring of 1963 provided anti-Diem Americans with the opportunity they had been awaiting. On June 11th, Buddhist monk Thich Quang Duc burned himself to death in the streets of Saigon, as an anti-Diem sacrifice. This was followed by agitation and demonstrations against the Diem Government by Buddhist groups. Halberstam and his colleagues had a field day with this, claiming large-scale discrimination against Buddhists by Diem and his entourage. Their attacks on Diem and his family became more bitter and scathing, to the point that most readers completely forget about the real problem — that of the Vietcong.

But not all correspondents saw things the same way that Mr. Halberstam did. Marguerite Higgins of the *New York Herald Tribune* traveled all over the country, but found little agitation over the "persecution" issue outside of Saigon and Hue. At the very pagoda in which a twenty-year-old monk had burned himself, Buddhists were unable to give her any concrete examples of their grievances.

Critics of Diem often used the invidious "Diem's *Catholic* government." Diem protested against this usage, asking why no one ever spoke in the same manner of "Kennedy's *Catholic* government." Overall, Diem's government was less Catholic than Kennedy's. Out of eighteen Vietnamese cabinet ministers at the time of the crisis, there were only five Catholics, and five Confucianists; there were eight Buddhists, including the Vice-President, Nguyen Ngoc Tho, and the Minister of Foreign Affairs, Vu Van Mau. Out of thirty-eight provincial governors, only twelve were Catholics; the remaining twenty-six were Confucianists or Buddhists. The governor of the town of Hue, where the most serious incidents occurred, was a Buddhist. Of nineteen top generals, three were Catholics; all the others were Confucianists, Taoists and Buddhists. The Commander-in-Chief, Le Van Ty, and the Saigon Military Governor, Ton That Dinh, were Buddhists. Seventy-five of the one-hundred thirteen members of Parliament were Buddhists.

In many ways the Buddhists were privileged. Catholic seminarists were required to fulfill the obligation of military service; bonzes were exempt. The Catholic Church was required to submit to the "Law on Associations", Ordinance No. 10, originated under Bao Dai; the Buddhist sect was not. President Diem, for having declined in 1957 to legislate equivalent scholastic privileges for Catholics, incurred the disfavor of many Catholics, who withheld their votes in the Presidential election. [1]

Under Vietnamese law, no religious group may fly religious flags over the national Vietnamese flag. This law was two years old when the so-called Buddhist crisis came to a head in May of 1963. In April, Catholic Archbishop Ngo Dinh Thuc consecrated the Redemporist Church in Hue and in deference to the law, flew the national flag and not the Vatican flag. Now it came time for the Buddhists to comply with the law. The Saigon Government reminded them of its provisions, in connection with the upcom-

[1] Labin, *op. cit.,* pp. 6, 7.

ing three day celebration of the birthday of Buddha, starting May 4, 1963. It also reminded the Catholics, in connection with the forthcoming Feast of the Ascension. But the bonzes wanted special treatment, and they made such a noise about it, that the Provincial Government of Hue, headed by Ngo Dinh Can (Diem's brother), yielded to their demands, and permitted all the Buddhist flags to be flown during the three-day celebration. The bonzes, who had been encouraged by the concessions, proceeded to make new demands that the law be repealed. They used the supposedly religious celebration for political purposes, and instead of following the program approved by the authorities, they organized a mass meeting at the national radio station and demanded the broadcast of their anti-Government demands in place of the original religious program. Meanwhile the crowd of demonstrators invaded houses and tear gas bombs were thrown to try to control the manifestation. But while the Provincial Chief, who had arrived at the radio station, was conferring with the chief bonze, part of the demonstrators went up the steps of the radio station, throwing rocks and breaking down the doors. At this moment an explosion (possibly a plastic bomb) killed seven persons on the steps, including two Catholic catechumens.

The bonzes profited from this tragic event, pinned the blame on the Provincial authorities, and made political hoopla out of the funerals, in spite of the protests of five of the families involved. Then the bonzes made certain demands on the Vietnamese Government, which were later taken up by the Buddhist Association of Vietnam. These included repeal of the flag law,

indemnification of the "victims who were un-
justly assassinated", with punishment "in a fitting
manner for those responsible," and a demand
that "the Government stop arresting and perse-
cuting the Buddhists." A United Committee for
the Defense of Buddhism was established (representing various sects) to realize the demands, to
fast in the Buddhist manner, and to make human
sacrifices. The Buddhist Association claimed to
represent 85% of the Vietnamese population, but
probably represented less than half this number
in fact.

The response of the Diem Government was to
create a ministerial commission headed by Vice
President Nguyen Ngoc Tho (a Buddhist), to
meet with the protesting Buddhists and try to
reach an understanding with them. Meetings
took place June 15-18, 1963. The Government
proceeded to give in to most of the Buddhist
demands, including adjudication of the flag issue, easing of regulations on the acquisition of
property, compensation for the families involved,
and several minor points. But then the Buddhists insisted that conclusion of an agreement of
conciliation must be based on the Government
assuming responsibility for the deaths in Hue.
The Government replied that it was precisely to
determine the responsibility of the events in Hue
that the joint investigating committee was being
established. The bonzes continued to insist on
their preliminary condition, and collaboration
became impossible.

Meanwhile the human sacrifices began. The
bonzes chose three old bonzes, and drew lots to
see which should be burned. They drugged him
and covered him with gasoline to burn him. "In
Hue we heard the screams of the bonze destined

to be burned at the Tu-Dum pagoda, the center of the General Buddhist Association. The bonze refused to die and the other bonzes overwhelmed him with hammer blows—this was the reason for the terrifying screams." [2] In this case as in others, the bonzes not only prevented the police and fire departments from putting an end to these horrors, but also refused to allow autopsies. Additionally, some of the anti-Diem newsmen, who were tipped off ahead of time by the bonzes about these human pyres, neglected to inform the authorities, who could have interceded and saved needless deaths.

In Saigon the aged monk Thich Quang Duc, the first publicly to perish in the flames, had been taken from a car and supported under the shoulders by two "friends" whom no one ever saw again. This creates the strong presumption that he had been drugged. The two holocausts that followed were voluntary, but were acts of youths whose parents testified that they had committed suicide from motives other than political. The fourth and fifth gratuitous martyrs seem actually to have been politically inspired.

But it does not follow that any of the suicides prove the justice of the anti-Diem cause. History is replete with ill-advised acts of heroism, like the Japanese suicide (kamikaze) pilots during World War II. For centuries tens of thousands of widows of the Buddhist faith have thrown themselves on funeral pyres to follow their older husbands in death. Bonzes often indulge in prolonged fasts which make them susceptible to hallucinations; suicide, far from being opposed

2 Archbishop Ngo Dinh Thuc, "What's Really Going on in Vietnam", *National Review,* November 5, 1963, p. 389.

by Buddhist dogma, has been openly advocated in some esoteric writings as a shorter route to Nirvana, preferably by fire because it is purifying.

The fact that there were seven additional suicides by fire *after* the coup that deposed Diem casts some doubt on the theory that the immolations were based on just Buddhist grievances against an oppressive "Catholic" government. But hardly any newsman was interested in the post-Diem immolations, for obvious reasons.

The day after the arrival of a UN Fact-Finding Mission, a young bonze, the sixth, was publicly consumed by flames. Suzanne Labin, in Saigon at the time, ascertained that two doctors had advised him that he would shortly die of tuberculosis.

Then, three days before the military coup against Diem broke out, a rumor circulated Saigon that a seventh bonze was going to commit suicide. The exact time and place was announced by telephone to selected newspaper reporters, twenty minutes before. "This", writes Miss Labin, "had become customary procedure." Without bothering to call the police to prevent the suicide, the anti-Diem newsmen proceeded to the gruesome tryst, in order to have another well carbonized corpse to throw in Diem's face--but this time their ghoulish anticipations were disappointed. The final act of the macabre drama was not played. The bonze was arrested, interrogated, and finally confessed. It turns out that he (Pham Bgoc Cam) was approached by the extremist Buddhists, and sold on a story of President Diem burning pagodas and torturing hundreds of bonzes to death. Poor Cam was then told that the Buddhist faith was threatened with total extinction—that the only way to save it was to make a public, dramatic, supreme sacrifice. If he would consent, he would have a "good chance" to be reincarnated as a Boddishatva, or even a Buddha. Otherwise he might well return as a dog or a snake. Young Cam was convinced that he should choose the faster, marvelous way of reaching his god and his heaven; death by fire.

As Miss Labin relates the story: "He was taken to Saigon and placed in reliable hands. He was provided with the modern instrument of the sacrifice: a plastic pan of kerosene, to be hidden under his robe in order to avoid arousing suspicion. The pan could be pierced with a knife, through his clothes, at the last moment before setting it afire. He was instructed to proceed very cautiously and to follow exactly a designated route to the place of his sacrifice, Boulevard Thong Nhut, behind the Cathedral. This spot had been chosen because many *foreigners*, and the members of the *United Nations Fact Finding Mission*, were scheduled to attend a celebration of the National Day on October 24. When the designated route was later retraced, it was obvious that it had been designed to be sure the poor, deceived bonze *would not pass by any pagoda* which he would have observed to be undamaged and visited peacefully by the faithful. The conspirators had not foreseen that, because of the celebration of National Day, some of the streets would be blocked. Cam therefore had to deviate from the prescribed route and suddenly found himself in front of *just such a pagoda*. He was deeply shocked. While he stood there, silent and overcome by dreadful misgivings, he was challenged by a police patrol. A cursory search revealed the kerosene pan hidden under his robe.

Taken immediately to a police station, he began confessing, though still reluctantly. A more intensive search yielded two *pinkish pills*. 'What was their purpose?' he was asked. 'They were,' he answered, '*poison* given to me to be swallowed when lighting the fire, so I could die without suffering.' And indeed, the pink color is that used in Vietnam to distinguish deadly poisons. Sent to the laboratory, the pills were soon identified as simply ... optalidon—a non-poisonous chemical! Poor Cam would not believe it, until a policeman ate some bits of the pills before his eyes. This finally brought about the collapse of Pham Ngoc Cam. He realized he had been framed and deceived, not only about the purported religious persecution, but also about the plans for *his own death*. This induced him to reveal the name of one of the conspirators who had approached him, who was shortly apprehended. He confirmed the whole sordid story and furnished the names of other bonzes who had been lured into this horrible trap. They were reached in time and saved.

The reason for the faked pills was obvious. The organizers of these induced suicides knew that poison was an essential inducement to overcome the normal human fear of the flames; however, they feared that it could be detected in the event a post-mortem examination was performed on the bodies. Therefore, in telling the ultimate lie to their victims, they were consciously sending them, not only to death, but to a most atrociously painful end. (Labin, *op. cit.,* pp. 23,24).

Human beings, these plotters?

The conclusion, then, is that the Buddhist agitation was political, not religious. Religion was dragged in by the heels, to belabor President Diem, to blacken his reputation, and to inflame world opinion. What did the Buddhists really want? In the words of Marguerite Higgins: "Diem's head... and not on a silver platter, but enveloped in the American flag."

There are two categories of bonzes. The first comprises those who officially practice celibacy and live in community. Many Vietnamese claim that only the lazy and incompetent become bonzes, because their upkeep is assured by the income of the pagodas. Their training, with the exception of a few men of letters, is almost nil. They learn by heart liturgical prayers in Pali which they recite without understanding, as do Catholic altar boys. The saffron yellow robe distinguishes them from laymen. The other category comprises the married bonzes who care for the small Buddhist sanctuaries scattered throughout the villages. Bonzes are chosen in a loose and superficial manner, which explains the behavior of certain individuals who wear the monastic habit without a vocation: they are the shame of the authentic bonzes who are highly respected by all Vietnamese.

The Communists, past masters at fishing in troubled waters, publicly took up the defense of Buddhism, speaking in the name of the "Democratic Republic of Vietnam," where almost all the pagodas have been destroyed and the bonzes assassinated or reduced to the state of slaves by the Communists. During the Korean war, some Buddhists were preaching that "to wipe out the American imperialist demons is not only blameless but meritorious." Ignoring the Chinese Communists' cruel persecution of Buddhism in Tibet, some Buddhists reason (as one scholar puts it) that when the Marxists' material needs are satisfied, they will "need something spiritual above and beyond," and that Buddhism will be able to supply it. This is the sort of self-delusion that led some bonzes and their followers into fellow-traveler paths. [3]

One of the reasons that the United States Government replaced Ambassador Frederick E. Nolting Jr., with Henry Cabot Lodge in mid-August, 1963, was because of Washington's displeasure with the way in which the Diem Government was handling the Buddhist protest movement. In the mounting strife between the Government and the dissident Buddhists, Washington for months sought to preserve an official neutrality. But when Diem cracked down on the political demonstrations c l o a k e d in religious terms, invaded the pagodas (which up to that time had had complete immunity from search and seizure) and arrested hundreds of bonzes, the Kennedy Administration, "in the coldly reproving tone which it reserves exclusively for friendly powers," condemned the Diem Government and took the side of the Buddhists. [4] The State Department charged that Diem had violated solemn pledges to pursue conciliatory policies toward its domestic opposition, and declared that it deplored oppressive measures.

But in view of the vast tolerance with which Washington generally views breaches of good faith by its enemies, its outrage with an ally seemed excessive. The encouragement it began to give to anti-Diem elements was an ominous portent for the future. The Diem Government,

[3] *Time,* August 23, 1963, p. 29.
[4] *Barron's,* August 26, 1963.

unlike some governments receiving more U.S. aid than Vietnam, was anti-Communist, honest, and friendly to Americans; the same cannot be said of many of its Vietnamese political foes, notably the Buddhists. To many observers the American Government began to embark on the same disastrous course of action it pursued in China between 1945 and 1949.

None other than Ambassador Nolting declared: "I myself—I say this after almost two and one-half years—have never seen any evidence of religious persecution." Marguerite Higgins reported that, "Nowhere in the countryside, which is constantly being circled by State Department reporters... is there religious persecution." Miss Higgins quoted a Buddhist as saying his leaders were keeping trouble alive "so American opinion will stay aroused." Writing in the *New York Herald Tribune* (August 27, 1963), she said: "It was Buddhist strategy, as a number of their leaders openly told me, to keep agitation - and publicity about it —at a high level until Washington finally 'ordered' new Ambassador Lodge somehow to remove the Diem family from power. A number of the now-jailed Buddhist leaders, in fact, asked me point blank: 'How much will it take to force the U.S. to act against Mr. Diem?' The Buddhist leaders are being persecuted all right - but for daring to challenge Mr. Diem, not for their religion." Indeed, the evidence was overwhelming that the disturbances were political rather than religious. Nevertheless the propaganda assault on the Diem regime was relentless. Late in June the *New York Times* carried a full-page advertisement captioned, "We Too Protest," signed by some clergymen active in the past with fellow-traveler groups. Featuring a gruesome picture of a Buddhist monk suffering self-immolation, the ad went on to protest, among other things: "Our country's military aid to those who denied him religious freedom; the immoral spraying of parts of South Vietnam with crop-destroying chemicals and the herding of many of its people into concentration camps called 'strategic hamlets'; the fiction that this is 'fighting for freedom.'" This appalling piece of copy elicited a prompt detailed rebuttal from a technician living in Vietnam, and led Representative Edna Kelly (D., N.Y.) who had recently been in Vietnam, to denounce it as a "flagrant example of distortion."

Referring to the self-immolated monk, the London *Economist* (June 15, 1963) commented: "The macabre incident... suggests a kind of religious fanaticism not normally associated with Vietnam. Coming at the end of six weeks of angry demonstrations by Buddhists it implies with much more certainty the unhappy instability of the society of South Vietnam and the consequent nervousness of its Government when faced with any opposition... Vietnam is not a Buddhist country as ... others in south-east Asia are. Such Buddhism as exists is weak and diffused, coming from the Mahayan Buddhism of China ... The most likely explanation of the conflict now being exploited by Vietnam's interested Buddhists is that it has the same character as those that broke out when President Diem first came to power in 1954. The Cao Dai and Hoa Hao, were two curious religious sects—the second an offshoot of Buddhism—both of which maintained private armies. Both were suppressed, contributing to the disaffection of the countryside which communist leadership now exploits. The current Buddhist opposition must be regarded as political rather than purely religious; certainly not as representative of any strength of religious following, but probably inflated by the discontent in a country where Government and people seem sadly out of contact with each other."

Thich Tri Quang was the Buddhist leader from Hue who was granted asylum at the American Embassy even though his past is in some controversy. According to records of the French Colonial Office, he had twice been arrested during the postwar French occupation of Indochina for dealings with Ho Chi Minh. By his own admission, he was a member of the Vietminh Communist Liberation Front. He claims to have fallen out with the Communists later. Again according to the French, who still have representatives at Hanoi, Thich Tri Quang's brother is currently working with Ho Chi Minh in the Communist Vietnam's Ministry of the Interior. The duties of Thich Tri Quang's brother are the direction of subversion in South Vietnam.

None of this, of course, proves anything about Thich Tri Quang's current attitude toward the Communist Vietcong. What does seem clear is that he learned a lot from the Communists about organization and propaganda. He ran his emergency headquarters at the Xa Loi pagoda like a company command post. Orders were barked out, directing a demonstration here, a protest meeting there. Messengers scurried in and out, carrying banners with their newly painted slogans. Respectful monks brought in the latest anti-Diem propaganda blast for Thich Tri Quang to review word by word.

In her discussion with Thich Tri Quang, Marguerite Higgins was somewhat taken aback at his indifference about the war against the Communists. When she asked whether the occasional outburst of turmoil might not offer the Vietcong the opportunity to infiltrate among the demonstrators Thich Tri Quang shrugged his shoulders and said: "It is possible that the current disorders could lead to Communist gains. But if this happens, it will be Diem's fault, not ours."

In the same interview in the Xa Loi pagoda, Thich Tri Quang told Miss Higgins that his preferred solution for Vietnam was "neutralism," adding: "We cannot get an arrangement with the North until we get rid of Diem and Nhu."[5]

The Buddhist label can be placed on a very heterogeneous religious alloy encompassing at most 35% of the population, having neither boundaries, gospels, sacraments, hierarchies, registers, or discipline. Suppose that fifteen villagers gathered around an improvised clay figure have a vision, or that they suddenly feel "love for all living creatures," so off they go, paint some ramshackle hut, place bent nails on the roof to ward off evil spirits, offer up a prayer, and there you have a Pagoda! A student, having shaved his head and donned a yellow robe, comes there to live the contemplative life, and there you have a bonze!

The informal Buddhist atmosphere makes it easy for the Communists to infiltrate. In her publication *Techniques of Communist Propaganda*, Suzanne Labin describes two Communist training schools in Tashkent, USSR, and Yunnan, China, where Buddhist lamas are trained to become agents of Communist subversion, so they

[5] *America,* January 4, 1964.

may enter the pagodas and transform them into seats of unrest, depots for tracts and weapons, centers of false rumors, and relays and refuges for saboteurs and terrorists. In Thailand, Cambodia, Nepal, and Japan, the authorities have had to arrest bonzes caught in the act of Communist subversion. A British authority on Buddhist matters, Mr. Holmes Welch, estimates that in Ceylon, where the government is particularly naive, 70% of the Buddhist monks are infected with Communism. In South Vietnam, large numbers of Buddhist monks attended a Communist Congress in the north early in 1963.[6]

Serious Communist penetration of the Buddhist monks in South Vietnam dates from the time that fellow traveler Thich Tri Quang established the militant "General Association of Buddhism," an originally minority offshoot of the largely nonpolitical National Sanka Association (Buddhist). The General Association (GAB) was established in Hue, and was from the start leftist in orientation. Quang chose Thien Tinh Khiet to head up the GAB. Khiet, a respectable and elderly man, neither reads nor writes.

Quang is a disciple of Thich Tri Do, one of the leaders of the Communist Buddhists in Hanoi. Quang's two living brothers both work for the Communist regime in the north: Thich Dien Minh was a member of the Quang Binh Communist Presidium in 1947 and occupies a top government job in Hanoi today; Pham Dai serves in a Communist military unit. A third brother, Pham Canh served as chief of a guerrilla unit until his death in 1947.

<hr>

[6]*National Observer,* September 2, 1963.

Quang created a flag for the GAB which many now accept as the Buddhist flag, and soon made it the emblem of anti-government demonstrations. He and his supporters have tried to get favored treatment for the GAB, hoping ultimately to make it the state religion.

When President Diem tried to enforce the ban on religious flags, Catholic groups abided by the rule, but not the GAB. It provoked the incident of May 8, 1963 in Hue, in cooperation with the Vietcong, claiming all the while that the Diem Government was suppressing the freedom of religion of Buddhists. On June 16th Diem, by this time subject to many pressures from outside Vietnam as well, made substantial concessions to the Buddhists, resulting in preferred treatment for them. But these concessions did not satisfy Quang, who had remained aloof in order to be able to ruin every effort to come to a reasonable solution, according to the Communist technique of "growing radicalization." Quang's party calls itself "Phat Giao Cap Tien", interpreted as "radical Buddhism." He and his acolytes continued the agitation, and were able to revive it in consequence of the Bonzes' dramatic immolations, which had such a powerful effect on world opinion. [7]

As the "Buddhist crisis" approached the crescendo, the Vietcong leader in Saigon issued the following instructions to all cadres: "Big Brother orders us to take in hand the control of the Buddhist movement, with the following objectives: 1) To widen our influence over the masses; 2) To compromise the government in the eyes of the country and of the world as a

[7]Labin, *op. cit.,* pp. 13-15.

persecutor; 3) To immobilize several fighting units in the towns. We must slowly but surely connect religious claims to more general expressions of opinion, in particular the immediate elimination of the strategic hamlets which we must ceaselessly depict as concentration camps. If necessary, we must ourselves initiate religious ceremonies, increase visits to bonzes and bonzesses, make the GAB armband more widely used, maintain the atmosphere of protest by young people and continual prayers in the pagodas... and keep the appearance of sustaining the Buddhist struggle." [8]

The immolations led to violence, forcing the Diem Government at long last to impose martial law, search the pagodas and arrest the conspiratorial bonzes. But the ringleader, Quang, was given refuge in the American Embassy by Henry Cabot Lodge. Meantime Khiet, President of the GAB, admitted that he had been taken in by the far Left, and venerable Thich Thien Hoa, President of the old Sangka, announced to his followers that the whole agitation had been artificial and invited genuine Buddhists to refrain from anti-government violence. He denounced the agitators as pursuing only political goals, and declared that he was taking over the administration of the pagodas.

The Army, although Buddhist in the majority, loyally supported the disciplinary action taken against the agitators. Indeed military leaders had for months been acutely aware of the machinations being contrived under shelter of certain pagodas, and had been pressing Diem to take action. On August 28, 1963, General Dinh, the

[8] *Ibid.*, pp. 16, 17.

Military Governor of Saigon, a Buddhist whose mother is a bonzess, held a press conference at which was exhibited everything seized in the pagodas: daggers, rifles, bombs, plastic moulds —even a mortar—and an impressive number of incriminating documents. But few Western journalists were interested. All that was newsworthy was the "Buddhist" agitation. These journalists, led by Halberstam, wanted to get rid of Diem. What contributed toward this end was newsworthy.

Close observers of the Vietnam scene had growing reason to suspect "that some Buddhist leaders, whatever their genuine grievances may be, are inspired less by religious than political fervor; that they have become either the tools, or the dupes, of the Chinese Communists." [9] This was the firm belief of the Honorable W. S. Kent Hughes, a former member of the Australian Parliament and longtime chairman of its foreign affairs committee. In a letter to the *Washington Post* early in August, 1963, Mr. Hughes cited some compelling evidence. In Ceylon, he pointed out, influential Buddhists openly avowed their support for a Communist regime. The same thing happened in Burma, where a "king-god from the Shan States has proclaimed a new kingdom among hill tribesmen in frontier jungles of North Laos and Northeast Thailand... The movement is directed and exploited by Chinese Communist agents." In Bangkok, the home of the South East Asia Treaty Organization, and capital of Thailand, "the authorities arrested two Buddhist priests on July 18 for subversive activities."[10] Nor was the State Department un-

[9] Barrons, *op. cit.*
[10] *Loc. Cit.*

aware of these and similar incidents; but it persisted in supporting the insurrectionists against the Government of Vietnam.

UN Secretary General U Thant, who likes to criticize non-Communist governments, criticized Diem's; the UN, which seldom concerns itself about violations of human rights in Communist countries, undertook to investigate the alleged maltreatment of Buddhists in Vietnam (South, not North). Ceylon's Ambassador Sir Senerat Guenwardena, neglecting to note that his own government has nationalized Catholic Schools and is forcing out Christian missionaries, charged President Ngo Dinh Diem with depriving Buddhists of "life, liberty, and security."[11] Somewhat to the surprise of the anti-Diem claque at the UN, Diem invited a UN mission to come to South Vietnam and see for itself if there was any violation of human rights in that country.

Meanwhile Buddhists from eleven Asian nations—some fellow-travelers but others apparently sincere monks—turned up in Peking for a three-day rally, listened to a Vietcong delegate denounce South Vietnam as "a hell on earth created by United States imperialism and its lackey, the Ngo Dinh Diem clique." Ignoring Red China's own subjugation of Buddhism, the meeting unanimously adopted a resolution accusing Diem of "atrocities." By serving as a vehicle for Red Chinese propaganda, the Buddhists hardly strengthened their case. [12]

The October 18, 1963 issue of *Time* declared that "Even Diem's severest critics in Saigon concede that there was no serious religious persecu-

[11] *Time,* October 18, 1963.
[12] *Time,* November 1, 1963, p. 36.

tion until the present troubles began, and that the Buddhist movement has become a political force dedicated to Diem's overthrow."

Contrary to misleading press reports, the Buddhists make up only about 30% of the Vietnamese population. There are five million Buddhists, 3.5 million Confucianists and followers of the Ancestors cult; 1.5 million Catholics, 1.5 million Cao Daists (who worship Joan of Arc, Sun Yat Sen and Victor Hugo), 0.5 million Protestants (mostly Baptists and Seventh Day Adventists), 0.5 million Hoa Haos, a cult of magic, one million pagan "montagnards," who worship spirits of the earth and winds; 0.5 million Hindus (worshipping Brahma and Vishnou); 0.3 million Muslims, and 0.5 million Taoists.

Impatient and even abusive demands for reform of our South Vietnamese ally in the fall of 1963 contrasted sharply with our lenient and tolerant view of our Communist enemy, whether he is brandishing missiles in Cuba, threatening to cut off Berlin, or kidnapping American citizens. In all the flurry of threats to our friends in Saigon, "No one seemed to be discussing perhaps the most sensible solution of all: stop halfway hints of encouragement to promoters of a coup d'etat and get on with the difficult...task of working with Ngo Dinh Diem and his family."[13]

If any mistake was made by the Ngos, it was in failing to take disciplinary action against the "Buddhists" sooner. People like Suzanne Labin urged Diem to refute the principal calumnies circulated against his government in Vietnam and in the world press. "My warnings, alas, were unheeded, probably because of the Presi-

[13] *Time,* September 20, 1963, p. 33.

dent's concept of the obligations imposed by his personal dignity and his under-estimation of the potentialities of Communist political warfare."[14]

The United Nations Mission which went to Vietnam to look into charges of Diem's suppressing the Buddhists found little evidence to support the charges. A Costa Rican member of the Mission, who had gone to Vietnam predisposed to accept the guilt of the Diem government declared: "The charges made in the General Assembly of the United Nations against the Diem government were not sustained... There was no religious discrimination or persecution... The clash between a small part–not all–of the Buddhist community and the Diem regime was on political grounds. I have the feeling that the majority of the Mission members (Afghanistan, Brazil, Ceylon, Costa Rica, Dahomey, Morocco and Nepal) share my conviction."[15]

[14] Labin, *op. cit.,* p. 19.
[15] *Ibid.,* p. 26.

CHAPTER NINE

1963: THE COUP AND THE MURDER

1963: The Coup and the Murder

President Ngo Dinh Diem's tough handling of
the Buddhist troublemakers, coming on top of
the removal of former Ambassador Nolting and
C.I.A. Chief John Richardson, led to a U.S.
policy of cold-shouldering the Diem Government,
and giving encouragement to anti-Diem plotters.
The U.S. Government absolved the South Vietnamese military of complicity in the suppression
of the Buddhist demonstrators, only to be em-
barrassed by a joint statement of leading generals that they *were* responsible.   Meantime,
the U.S. Embassy gave asylum to several Buddhist monks (later the Embassy denied asylum
to Hue Governor Ngo Dinh Can, and turned
him over to the mercy of the triumphant military junta).   The new U.S. Ambassador, Henry
Cabot Lodge, pointedly had a conference with
these monks before making his first call on
President Diem.

Reports of U.S. support of a coup d'etat
against the South Vietnamese Government now
began to gain more frequency. On September 9,
1963, *Newsweek* declared: "There is no guarantee that if the U.S. engineers a military coup
against the (Diem) family, as it *is plainly hop-*

ing to do, that the new regime will prosecute the war more vigorously and with the same sense of purpose that, in the early days at least, had inspired Diem and his tightly knit family group." *Business Week* (August 31, 1963) carried the following headline: "U.S. May Pull Rug From Under Diem", followed by this sub-head: "we may even back a military coup." This liberal publication proceeded to charge that "Diem's persecution of the Buddhists is sapping resistance to the Communist Vietcong." This and similar charges were immediately contra-dicted by American military men in Saigon, and by Vietnamese military victories over the Vietcong, notably that at Cai Nuoc (Camau peninsula) in mid-September.[1] *The Business Week* article said in part: "Washington made it clear that it no longer would support the re-gime of Ngo Dinh Diem in its present form. Implicit in this position was another - if it takes a military coup to stop Diem's repression...the U.S. is for it." Two weeks previously there was a report that "one top Vietnamese official secretly in contact with army dissidents maintains that a coup can and will be staged, that both marines and the air force would join in any uprising, and that there are enough disaffected forces in Saigon itself to neutralize Tung's Special Forces."[2]

On August 24, Ambassador Lodge, newly arrived in Saigon, received a cable from the State Department suggesting various courses of action for the U.S. Government, among them a U.S.-backed coup to depose President Diem. The

[1] *Time,* September 20, 1963.
[2] *Time,* September 6, 1963, p. 20.

message was not shown, as it should have been, to a Pentagon official high enough to understand its explosive implications. If it had been, it probably would never have left Washington, because the Defense Department never did buy the State Department view that victory over the Vietcong was impossible so long as the Diem Government remained in power. The Pentagon position was: fight the Communists, not the Diem family.

In direct opposition to this was a small but determined core of State Department "doves," known around Washington as the "Gung Ho Boys," who "sometimes seem more interested in overthrowing the heavy-handed Diem regime than in pushing the war against the Viet Cong."[3] Among the leaders of this leftist clique was Roger Hilsman, Assistant Secretary of State for Far Eastern Affairs. Admired by his friends at State as an "independent thinker," his Pentagon critics have dubbed him "the field marshal," because, they say, he tried to run the whole military-political war in Vietnam. And who was the author of the August 24 cable? None other than Roger Hilsman.

That such an incendiary message should ever have been sent without the approval of the Pentagon "seems astonishing."[4] Yet it was sent, with the approval of Under Secretary of State, Averill Harriman. Harriman is an acknowledged expert on Kremlin affairs, but some career Foreign Service Officers consider him a rank amateur on the subject of Southeast Asia, and point to his failure of Laos as an example.

[3] *Time,* October 4, 1963.
[4] *Loc. cit.*

Among the many Pentagon officials who were enraged by this message was Defense Secretary McNamara, whose indignation, "while it lasted, ...was an atomic blast."[5]

Hilsman denied that the United States was planning a coup d'etat, but evidence to the contrary was mounting. On the night of August 24-25, a State Department statement was broadcast to the fronts in Vietnam. The statement was interpreted as urging the troops remaining in battle to repudiate the leadership of Diem and his family. The troops refused.[6]

Meantime, two powerful Congressional Democrats told President Kennedy that the United States would court disaster if the Diem Government was weakened or overthrown by withholding U.S. aid. In an apparent effort to counter the influence of Hilsman and Company, Speaker John McCormick and Representative Edna Kelly urged the President not to become a party of the anti-Diem conspiracy. In 1955 the same two successfully teamed up to block a similar State Department effort to oust Diem.

McCormick and Kelly stressed that "inaccurate and erroneous information" on the South Vietnam leader's internal dispute with the Buddhists was being circulated by the press and by some State Department officials to the detriment of the Diem Government. The legislators urged the President to examine personally the evidence obtained by Vietnamese security forces indicating Communist infiltration of Buddhist ranks. Representative Kelly reminded the President: "Almost no one bothers to point out that, faced with insurmountable obstacles, with his country torn

[5] *Loc. cit.*
[6] *Counterattack,* October 11, 1963, p. 167.

apart and overrun by Communists, bandits, and warring sects, President Diem not only has managed to survive for nine years but has made considerable progress in bringing order, freedom, justice, and opportunity for a better life to most of his nation. No one bothers to point out that without him, the one element of stability present in Vietnam could disappear, plunging Vietnam and all of Indochina into chaos, completely undermining our position in that strategic part of the globe."[7]

Whether President Kennedy took this advice to heart is not known, although he did assure both legislators that their views would be given consideration as part of the overall review then being made of U.S. policy toward Vietnam. Most of the review consisted in sending General Maxwell Taylor and Defense Secretary McNamara to Vietnam to evaluate our position. Their report was ambiguous, although in the main implying confidence in the ability of the Diem Government to achieve military victory over the Communists.

According to *Washington World* (October 14, 1963), one of the key men in the Hilsman "Gung Ho" anti-Diem clique was Paul M. Kattenburg, director of the State Department's "Working Group for Vietnam." Indeed this article states that "As was the case in 1955, the U.S. official masterminding the move to oust Diem" was Kattenburg. A former World War II official in the OSS and a naturalized citizen from Belgium, Kattenburg first tried to oust Diem in 1955 while he was in charge of the Department's office of Vietnam Affairs, according to Con-

[7] *The Washington World,* October 14, 1963, p. 8.

gressional sources that successfully opposed that effort. In July, 1963, Kattenburg popped up in the key post of the Vietnam Working Group after being shifted from the Foreign Service Language School. "Since his return to Vietnam policy-making, Kattenburg has pushed for a full-scale review of U.S. activities in South Vietnam and the ouster of Diem."[8] According to one reliable State Department source, Kattenburg contended that the price of a military victory over the Communists was higher than American vital interests could justify.

By mid-October, the general trend of the Administration's revised thinking about Vietnam became clearer. It suspended its subsidy to the elite 2,000 member Vietnamese Special Forces, and stopped the 12 million dollar a month program of paying for imported U.S. foodstuffs and manufactured goods. (About this same time, the U.S. Government decided to make wheat available to Hungary and the Soviet Union to alleviate food shortages in those Communist countries.) Almost immediately, there were bad effects. As fear of future food shortages spread, hoarding set in and prices jumped. Sugar, textiles, and tires vanished from the shelves, and the Vietnamese piaster, normally worth 73 to the dollar was being traded for as much as 160. All this produced a sullen mood on the part of Saigon's people, sometimes directed at the Diem regime, sometimes against the Americans. On the eve of National Day, marking the eighth anniversary of the formation

[8]*Loc. cit.*

of South Vietnam, rumors of an uprising became rife. [9]

Thursday, October 31, the Government of South Vietnam announced that it was planning to release Buddhist leaders arrested during raids on the pagodas August 21. President Diem was preparing to make conciliatory moves toward Ambassador Henry Cabot Lodge and the United States Government; indeed Lodge declared that he was confident that things would improve. But now it was too late. Forces had already been set in motion which could not be stopped without positive United States action.

For months "coup" had been the loudest whisper heard in South Vietnam. Coup is what correspondents and some U.S. officials talked about in the bar at the Hotel Caravelle. Coup is what President Diem and his Government feared; coup is what certain generals finally plotted. These generals had heard President Kennedy say, in mid-October that the winning of the war against the Communist Vietcong would probably require "changes in policy, and perhaps in personnel" in the Diem Government. They had observed the cut in U.S. aid, and the bitter attacks by some U.S. officials and newsmen. When Madame Ngo Dinh Nhu, then visiting Los Angeles declared: "There will be no coup without American incitement or backing," even her severest critics, including the Moscow press, agreed with her.

"Hell, there's been so much advance knowledge we can't possibly imagine why the Diem government didn't know, too," said one high

[9] *Time,* November 1, 1963, p. 36.

U.S. official. [10]   Writing in the *New York Times* (Nov. 2, 1963), Max Frankel reported that "Though officials denied direct involvement in the plot, they had reached the conclusion that South Vietnam and the war effort would profit from the overthrow of President Ngo Dinh Diem and, especially, of his domineering brother and chief advisor, Ngo Dinh Nhu." Mr. Frankel then wrote: "Washington recognized its large share of responsibility for the coup and its stake in the action's success." "We wanted a change in the way this country was being run," said a top U.S. diplomat in Saigon. "If those in power couldn't change their ways, then we favored changing those in power." [11]

In the week that followed the violent anti-Buddhist raids, the plotting insurgents in Vietnam were greatly heartened by strong signs of U.S. distaste for the Diem regime. President Kennedy had made it clear that he disapproved of the Ngo Dinh family. The U.S. aid to Vietnam was curtailed, and Ambassador Lodge grandly told Diem that his brother Nhu was undesirable. And the CIA chief in Saigon, John Richardson, the man in the American mission closest to brother Nhu, was summarily called home.

But none of these encouraging gestures made the mechanics of revolt any easier, and the insurgent generals began to work out another design. This time they concentrated on winning over the loyal General Ton That Dinh. A courageous but not very bright soldier, Dinh's fidel-

[10] *Time,* November 8, 1963, p. 21.
[11] Stanley Karnow, "The Fall of the House of Ngo Dinh", *Saturday Evening Post,* December 21-28, 1963, p. 76.

ity to Diem was exceeded only by his monumental egocentricity. The generals played on this fatal weakness.

They softened Dinh up with flattery, telling him that he was a personage of historic proportions, and they even bribed an astrologer to depict an important political future for him.

By October 29 Dinh was apparently in the rebel fold. General Dinh's first problem was to evacuate Diem's four loyal Special Forces companies from the capital. He explained to Diem's faithful Special Forces commander, Col. Le Quang Tung, that fresh troops would have to be brought into Saigon to replace them. Next day, with Diem's approval, the Special Forces left Saigon. A major obstacle to the coup d'etat was thus removed. Now Dinh's job was to deploy his forces for the revolt.

Diem's disaster struck on All Saint's Day. After attending Mass, President Diem conferred with Ambassador Lodge and Admiral Harry Felt, commander of U.S. forces in the Far East, who had arrived in Saigon for a "routine visit" and planned to leave for Hong Kong later in the morning. Whether Lodge and Felt knew what was about to happen is not clear. There had been inklings of a coup, including rumors that the anti-Diem generals had begun to move loyal troops away from the capital. David Halberstam of the *New York Times*, who had led the anti-Diem cabal of reporters, received a slip of paper the night before with the message: "Please buy me one bottle of whisky at the PX." This was a pre-arranged signal meaning that a coup might be imminent. [12]

---

[12] *Ibid.,* p. 28.

With Diem and Nhu under the illusion that he was preparing for their protection, Dinh rapidly shifted troops in and out of Saigon. D-day was Friday, November 1; H-hour was 1:30 P.M. Throughout the preceding night and following morning the insurgent legions rushed to take up their position.

By midmorning of November 1, the whole area around Saigon was in stealthy movement, and no single person knew precisely what was happening everywhere. At about nine A.M. for example, Diem's loyal navy commander, Capt. Ho Tan Quyen, was met by two subordinates who came to give him birthday greetings. Instead, they asked him to join the revolt, and when he refused, they drove him outside town and shot him.

American military advisers, who live with the Vietnamese army, were well aware that a revolt was in the making, and those attached to General Dinh's staff knew the exact time it would begin. They reported the information to their headquarters, but the U.S. commander, Gen. Paul Harkins, apparently did not believe the news. Ambassador Henry Cabot Lodge was probably less skeptical, however. At 10 A.M. he took visiting Adm. Harry Felt, commander in chief of the U.S. Pacific forces, to see Diem for an hour. It was an odd confrontation. Both Lodge and Diem knew that a major event was in the offing, and they discussed "rumors" of a revolt.

Shortly after 1 P.M. rebel units threw road blocks across the avenues leading from the city to Saigon airport, while truckloads of insurgent marines raced toward the heart of downtown Saigon. Pro-Diem units at police headquarters, navy headquarters, and at the telegraph office and radio station were overwhelmed. A particularly fierce battle developed at navy headquarters where loyalist units fought back, even after being subjected to strafing attacks from rebel planes. By 4:45 P.M. the Saigon radio was in rebel hands, and it broadcast a general revolutionary appeal signed, among others, by General Tran Van Don. Don had dined with Admiral Felt the night before, and had seen the Admiral off at the airport shortly before the shooting started. In the presidential palace Diem and Nhu fully believed that General Dinh was loyal to them and would, as calculated, turn on the plotters and take the situation in hand.

As the afternoon wore on, however, Diem and his brother slowly began to sense that something was going wrong. A bit past 4 P.M. insurgent artillery opened fire on his presidential-guard barracks, and Diem knew he was in trouble. He telephoned Ambassador Lodge to tell him that the army was rebelling. Coolly acknowledging that he had heard some shooting, Lodge expressed his concern for Diem's welfare and reminded him that the rebels had offered him a safe conduct out of the country. "I shall try to restore order," snapped Diem. Replied Lodge, "If there's anything I can do to assure your personal safety, let me know."

About 8:00 P.M., with the palace surrounded, Diem and Nhu fled through a tunnel that took them to a wooded area near the Cercle Sportif, Saigon's sporting club. At the tunnel exit, a confederate was waiting to drive them to the home of a Chinese merchant, Ma Tuyen. The house had a direct link with the palace telephone. Neither the insurgent forces attacking it nor the troops defending it ever knew that night they were fighting for an empty palace.

In their new hideout in the Chinese district of Cholon, Diem and Nhu still hoped that General Dinh would rescue them, and they doggedly continued to telephone him. It was past midnight when, for the first time that day, they reached him directly at the Joint General Staff headquarters. With the other insurgents beside him, Dinh was apparently anxious to dispel any doubts about his allegiance to the rebel cause. Using a choice lexicon of Vietnamese obscenities, he barked at Diem: "Dinh saved you m-----rs many times, but not now, you b-----s. You s-----s are finished. It's all over."

As the rebels gradually gained the upper hand, they encircled the Presidential palace. Diem broadcast appeals to loyal troops to keep up the fight: "We shall not give in," he cried. But the rebels had planned too well, and most of the loyal units were far away from Saigon. At 9:45 P.M. units launched a mortar and artillery barrage against the palace guard barracks. By midnight a force of eighteen tanks supported by armored cars surrounded the palace. At 4:00 A.M., from several side streets, the attacking columns began pouring point blank fire— from tanks, cannons, machine guns and rifles— into the palace walls. Back came a murderous counterfire, everything Diem's defenders had left. At 6:15 A.M. the final push came, and shortly thereafter, the defending forces raised the white flag. Rebel soldiers then rushed into the palace, manhandling and abusing the loyal soldiers, looting, and smashing furniture.

By about 8:30 A.M. Cholon was fully awake and bustling. Diem and Nhu decided to seek sanctuary in the church of St. Francis Xavier. There may have then been some contact - possibly by telephone — between Diem and Nhu and the revolutionaries. Either that or they were betrayed.

Within minutes, three armored cars were dashing across the city. At about 9:45 they pulled into the narrow, dead-end street facing the church. Personally commanding them was Gen. Mai Huu Xuan. A high police official in the French colonial administration, Xuan had been shunted into a minor job by Diem, and he detested the president. He was a poor choice for this delicate mission. But he was the only man who dared accept it. Asked to accompany Xuan, another general declined, saying, "Diem doesn't deserve two generals."

Despite the bitterness of their fight against him, the insurgents could not shake off their respect for Diem. When the armored cars arrived at the church, the rebels hesitated to arrest the president and his brother immediately. Instead, they sent in a once-loyal officer to lure them out. At the sight of a faithful subordinate, Diem and Nhu emerged. The rebel troops promptly seized them. They tied the brothers' hands behind their backs and unceremoniously pushed them into one of the armored cars.

For some inexplicable reason, General Xuan did not ride with Diem and Nhu. The vehicle that carried them was commanded by a tall, swarthy tank-corps major once connected with the Dai Viet party, a dissident movement that opposed both Diem and the Communists. According to some insiders, the major burned with desire to avenge a close friend whom Nhu had executed.

"As we rode back to the Joint General Staff headquarters," an eyewitness told Stanley Karnow, "Diem sat silently, but Nhu and the major began to insult each other. I don't know who started it. The name-calling grew passionate. The major had hated Nhu before. Now he was charged with emotion. Suddenly he lunged at Nhu with a bayonet and stabbed him again and again, maybe fifteen or twenty times. Still in a rage, he turned to Diem, took out his revolver and shot him in the head. Then he look back at Nhu, who was lying on the floor, twitching. He put a bullet into his head too. Neither Diem nor Nhu ever defended themselves. Their hands were tied."[13]

When the armored cars reached staff headquarters with the two bodies, the generals were aghast. They had not the slightest sympathy for Nhu. But for all their impatience with his policies, they had always been awed by Diem's courage and stature. Besides, they had promised him safety and now their own honor was betrayed. One of them wept openly, and General Dinh said later, "I couldn't sleep that night."

To cover their obvious sense of guilt, the generals first claimed that Diem and Nhu had committed suicide, a tale that was later amended to "accidental suicide." Privately, they admitted that Diem and his brother had been murdered. Adding to the mystery, they refused to state publicly where the bodies were buried. They are

---

[13]The major was later identified as Nguyen Van Nhung, loyal aide to Maj. Gen. Duong Van Minh, who stepped into power as the leader of the military junta the day of the assassination.

believed to lie in a prison cemetery near Saigon airport.[14]

Ngo Dinh Diem, Father of his Country, the last of the Mandarins, described by Lyndon Baines Johnson in 1961 as the "Winston Churchill of Asia", had crossed to the other side.

[14]*Ibid.,* p. 78.

CHAPTER TEN

A POST MORTEM

Excerpts from Marguerite Higgins, "Saigon Summary," *America,* January 4, 1964, pp. 18-21, reprinted with permission.

A Post Mortem

What is the meaning of the five tragic self-immolations that took place in Vietnam in the six weeks following the November coup d'etat against Diem? How did it come to pass that under the military junta, which seized power in the name of an end to "persecution", there have been more suicides by fire over a short period than had ever been the case under President Diem and his brother Ngo Dinh Nhu? Even though virtually ignored by the Western press, will this latest spate of suicides by fire - without clearly stated reason - destroy at last the false notion that the repeated acts of self-immolation in Vietnam were indisputable proof of massive persecution of the Buddhist religion by President Diem, a Roman Catholic?

Will historians be more equitable with President Diem than his contemporaries were?

On two trips in Vietnam in 1963, one before and one after the coup d'etat, this writer was never able to find an instance of repression on religious grounds. Under Diem, there was repression of Buddhists, Catholics, Confucianists, etc., when - in defiance of clearly stated laws - they took to the streets to demonstrate against the government. But Diem's repression was not directed against a religion. It was aimed at overt political opposition. There were deplorable police excesses in Vietnam, but there is no sign that they were desired or condoned by Diem any more than police excesses in Alabama are condoned or desired by Washington.

There was, for a long time, a clear double standard in Vietnam, in which accusations against Diem gained, in most cases, giant headlines, but attempted refutations received only perfunctory notice. For instance, last summer, Thich Duc Nghiep, the Xa Loi pagoda spokesman, told reporters dramatically that 365 persons in Saigon suburb had been arrested "because they were Buddhists." That figure was headlined throughout the world. But when I went to the suburb in question I found that a routine check was being made of a neighborhood through which the Vietcong often infiltrated. I stayed for two hours to talk with those rounded up as they emerged from the police compound after questioning. I talked to 20 persons—ancestor worshipers, Catholics, Confucianists, Taoists, Caodaists, etc.—before I finally found a genuine Buddhist among those picked up. So the charge of "365 persons arrested because of being Buddhists" was invention.

There is no doubt that the overwhelming majority of the American press corps in Saigon thought — out of the most idealistic and patriotic motives — that they were serving a good cause in arousing world opinion against Diem. Whether his strengths and faults were greater or less than those of his junta successors remains to be seen.

It is certain that under the military junta, Vietnamese have been jailed for far less than was necessary to send a person to prison under Diem. Said a European observer: "Under Diem, a Vietnamese had to do something specific against the regime to get into trouble. Under the military junta, a Vietnamese can be jailed without charge, simply under the suspicion that he was loyal to the Diem regime when it was the legally constituted authority."

Sanche de Gramont, of the *New York Herald Tribune*, has estimated the number of arbitrary arrests right after the coup as around 500. So far, Mr. de Gramont and this reporter are the only ones who have written with any detail about the junta's reversion to some of the police state tactics the Saigon press corps so bitterly criticized in Diem.

Nowadays, some of the most ardent anti-Diem writers, such as David Halberstam, Saigon correspondent of the *New York Times*, acknowledge that the Buddhist agitation of last summer and fall was politically motivated. In an admiring magazine article written by his close friend George J. W. Goodman, Mr. Halberstam is quoted as saying: "I always said it. The Buddhist campaign was political... I thought I always emphasized that this was a political dispute under a religious banner - the only place an opposition had found to gather in an authoritarian regime..."

Whatever Mr. Halberstam's intentions, his and other press dispatches last summer and fall did create the impression in the outside world that some kind of religious crisis was going on inside Vietnam. And it was the image of religious persecution —false as it was— that paved the way for Diem's downfall. Without the embarrassment of being the patron of a country suspected of battling Buddhists, it is doubtful that the United States would ever have reached the decision to try to get rid of Diem. The authorities in Washington knew, of course, that the conflict in Vietnam was political, not religious. But they were reluctant to speak out lest, in the process, they attract to Washington some of the onus being poured — with hardly any contradiction — on Diem.

By staying silent, Washington acted as if it thought Diem guilty. And this helped to complete the vicious circle.

Or as Roger Hilsman, Assistant Secretary of State for Far Eastern Affairs put it: "After the closing of the pagodas on August 21, the facts became irrelevant." So, evidently, did a sense of perspective. What, for example, about the fact that President Diem was far more lenient to his political opposition than President Sukarno of Indonesia or Premier Sarit Thanarat of Thailand, both recipients of American aid? Whereas some 300 political prisoners, at most, were found in Diem's jails, the prisons of Thailand, Indonesia and Burma were filled — and are still filled — with tens of thousands of political victims.

"But," explained a pro-coup State Department officer, "the world spotlight is not on those countries, and it is on Vietnam."

At the State Department, there have been some attempts to rationalize the coup d'etat by describing it as necessary to save the Vietnamese war effort from going to pieces. One difficulty with this argument is that it makes liars out of Secretary of Defense McNamara, Chief of Staff Maxwell D. Taylor and Gen. Paul Harkins, who testified under oath to Congress in October that the war was making reasonable progress. If the

State Department ever took seriously the argument that the disturbances in the cities would affect morale in the countryside, it betrays a regrettable lack of understanding of the structure of Vietnam and of the gap between the countryside, where the war will be won or lost, and the cities, where less than ten percent of the Vietnamese live.

For the Buddhists, intellectuals and students who marched the streets in anti-Diem demonstrations could not have cared less about the war—before the coup, or after the coup. Vietnamese students in particular tell you quite frankly that one reason they prize admission to a university is that it enables them to avoid the draft. Vietnam's intellectuals have narrow horizons, are excessively inward-turning, and make constant and factional criticism their specialty. Except for a handful of terribly militant leaders, Buddhist monks are rather passive. If the success or failure of the war were to depend on these groups, Vietnam would have been lost from the start. As to the effects in the countryside of the critical clamoring by Vietnam's spoiled young intellectuals in the cities, it was virtually nil. The American attitude seemed to be that if a Vietnamese student demonstrates, virtue is on his side, and the government is wrong. But in the countryside there were many peasants and plain soldiers who disapproved of the defiance of the regime — in those rare places where anyone knew anything whatsoever of what went on beyond the next village.

If there was any slowdown in the war in September and October of 1963, it was because the Vietnamese generals—under American prodding–were concentrating on thoughts of a coup d'etat while Diem and Nhu, out of fear of America, were concentrating on how to prevent a coup.

It was not until after the coup d'etat that the Vietnamese war took a decidedly downward turn. The military junta with its uncertain leadership, after purges of key (and scarce) officials, finally plunged much of the countryside into the confusion from which it purportedly was trying to save Vietnam.

No wonder the Vietcong took advantage of the situation to seize the military initiative for the first time in many months. No wonder that, in two months after the coup d'etat, the military junta lost more real estate, lives and weapons to the Vietcong than at any previous time in the war.

It was precisely out of fear of such predictable consequences of trying to change regimes in mid-war that Secretary of Defense McNamara and Central Intelligence Agency Director John McCone opposed a coup d'etat faction led by Ambassador Henry Cabot Lodge, Undersecretary of State Averell Harriman, and Assistant Secretary of State for Far Eastern Affairs Roger Hilsman.

The Diem-must-go decision came shortly after the temporary closing of about a dozen (out of 4,000) pagodas on August 21, which outraged Washington. Diem said that his only aim was to get the Buddhist leaders out of politics and back to religion. The Vietnamese leader insisted that unless he shut down the propaganda machinery of the pagodas and put a halt to the glorification of suicide by burning, public disorder in the cities would mount and world misunderstanding would deepen. Washington disagreed. Further, it felt that Diem had not only humiliated it and flouted its advice, but had broken a promise to be conciliatory. Washington's anger was heightened by horrendous stories of alleged killings and brutalities during the pagoda raids. (There were no such killings, as the monks themselves later said.)

In any case, on August 24, the State Department sent out word — without the knowledge of Secretary McNamara or of C.I.A. Director John McCone — instructing Ambassador Lodge to "unleash" the Vietnamese generals with a view to toppling the Diem Government if they could. Plotting among educated Vietnamese, including the generals, is a kind of national pastime, as chess is to the Russians. Until lately it had been a pretty harmless pastime, because everybody knew that real action was dependent on an American green light — and until August such a green light had been withheld.

But on Sunday, August 25, Washington publicly gave the generals a green light in a Voice of America broadcast that virtually called on the Vietnamese military to take over. At the same time, Ambassador Lodge asked the C.I.A. to poll the Vietnamese generals and see when and if they were ready to translate revolt talk into action.

Diem's shock at the Voice of America broadcast and the C.I.A. poll of the Vietnamese generals can only be imagined by turning the tables around. Suppose the United States were engaged in a war against the Communists in which we depended almost totally on aid from Vietnam; suppose, in the middle of that war, Vietnam issued a broadcast calling for the American Joint Chiefs of Staff to overthrow the American government?

The miracle is that the Diem regime survived as long as it did the virtual declaration of political war served on it that August by Washington.

What, after many months of hesitation, finally decided the generals (in mid-October) to stage the coup? In separate interviews with this correspondent, members of the military junta spoke of these factors:

1. The late President Kennedy called, at a press conference, for "changes of policy and maybe personnel" in Vietnam.

2. Washington announced the withdrawal of 1,000 American soldiers by the end of 1963, and possible total withdrawal by 1965. (Said one general: That convinced us that unless we got rid of Diem, you would abandon us.)

3. The economic aid was cut. Many generals agreed that this cut was psychologically the most decisive goad to a coup d'etat. "It convinced us," a key plotter explained, "that the United States was serious this time about getting rid of Diem. In any case this was a war we wanted to win. The United States furnished us with the jeeps, the bullets, the very guns that made the war possible. In cutting economic aid, the United States was forcing us to choose between your country's help in the war and Diem. So we chose the United States."

Ironically, President Diem did make some important concessions to the United States in September and October. For example, in mid-September President Diem agreed to every point put forward by the United States in a program to reform and consolidate the strategic hamlet program in the Mekong delta. Many Americans had long felt that this program had been over-extended. At last President Diem agreed with the diagnosis and decided to do something about it. Why was this move toward the American position never publicized? One Western diplomat put it this way: "Ambassador Lodge and his deputy, William Truehart, were so determined to get rid of Diem that they were opposed to putting him in a conciliatory light. They were afraid this would strengthen the hands of those in Washington against a coup d'etat."

Even at the eleventh hour, Ambassador Lodge could, of course, have turned off the revolt if he had chosen to give the slightest sign that the New Frontier and President Diem were even beginning to move to heal their rent. As one member of the military junta put it: "We would never have dared to act if we had not been sure that the United States was giving us its moral support."

In the last hours before his death, President Diem was stripped of any doubt whatsoever of Washington's hostility. Telephoning the American Embassy from the Palace at 4:30 P.M. on November 1, after the bombardment had started, President Diem asked Ambassador Lodge; "What is Washington's attitude toward this?" Lodge replied: "I don't know Washington's attitude. After all, it is four-thirty in the morning there."

"But you must have some idea," Diem said. Whereupon Lodge turned the conversation to the matter of Diem's safety, offering him an airplane to take him out of the country. Could anything have indicated more clearly that in American eyes the success of the coup d'etat was a fait accompli?

The only certain thing about the murder of President Diem and Counselor Nhu is that they were shot in the back (Diem in the neck, Nhu in the right side) with their hands tied behind them. Nhu also had a dagger or bayonet wound in the chest, which was apparently indecisive.

These facts were established beyond all doubt by this reporter through photographs and through talks with military eyewitnesses, attendants at St. Paul's Hospital (where the bodies were first taken) and from information given by two relatives, a niece and nephew who handled the preparations for the burial.

In the light of the way Diem and Nhu died, there is a strong possibility that the shootings were ordered by some or all of the military junta. Would a junior officer take such a responsibility on himself?

Now for the Buddhist leaders who started it all: have they got what they wanted? I use the word "leaders" advisedly, for of the Buddhists in Vietnam, who form about 30 percent of the population of 14 million people, the overwhelming majority are largely nonpolitical. Buddhist monks tend to be somewhat passive. They would never have dreamed of resorting to violent demonstrations had they not been subjected to the skillful and inflammatory propaganda that poured from the humming mimeograph machines of the Xa Loi pagoda. By the end of last summer, the original grievances of the Buddhist leaders in Hue—matters of property rights, flag flying, etc. — had largely been met by the Diem regime.

In the midst of the anti-Diem ferment I wrote an article asking: "What do the Buddhists want? They want Diem's head—not on a silver platter, but wrapped in an American Flag."

You have to hand it to the Buddhist leaders that they got what they wanted. But will this satisfy the more militant Buddhist leaders? It is heady stuff, even for Buddhists, to have the attention of the entire world focused on you, and to exercise the kind of political power than can topple governments. Will, for instance, the venerable Thich Tri Quang, the mastermind of the Buddhist campaign and by far the most intelligent and militant of all, be satisfied to take a political back seat?

CHAPTER ELEVEN

WHERE NEXT VIETNAM?

Where Next Vietnam?

"The murder of Vietnam's President Ngo Dinh Diem last November in a coup encouraged by the United States had a disastrous effect upon U.S. repute throughout Asia. This assassination was one of the blackest moments in the history of American diplomacy. We cannot dodge responsibility for what happened." (Richard Nixon, "Needed in Vietnam: The Will to Win," *Readers' Digest*, August, 1964, page 38).

Madame Nhu, whose husband was murdered in the U.S.-inspired revolt, said, "If you have the Kennedy Administration for an ally, you don't need an enemy." This tragic woman may have done her brother-in-law more harm than good with her acid tongue, but she said many truthful things. While our government honored Tito, Secretary of State Rusk berated our press for giving Madame Nhu a platform. Certainly our support of Souvanna Phouma in Laos over the anti-Communist Phoumi Nosavan, our initial welcome of Castro's triumph, our approval of the Communist-inspired terrorists in Angola over Portugal, and our refusal to support Portugal against Indian aggression, our support of the imperialist Sukarno over the Dutch, our support of UN aggression against Katangan self-determination—might well be cited in support of Madame Nhu's bitter charge.

We refused to recognize anti-Communist military juntas in Peru, the Dominican Republic, and Honduras, but we hastened to recognize the military junta that overthrew "the Winston Churchill of Asia." Most shocking of all, was the almost total lack of outrage expressed by both the Kennedy Administration and the press.

Cries of strong revulsion against the assassinations finally came, not from any government official in Washington, but from two liberal Democratic lawmakers. Senate Majority Leader Mike Mansfield (D.-Mont.) said he was "shocked and grieved" to hear of Diem's murder. Diem, he confided, was "an old and valued friend." He was, Mansfield concluded "a man of great integrity and great patriotism. It is sad, indeed, that such a situation has come to pass."

Rep. Clement Zablocki (D.-Wis.), a member of the House Foreign Affairs Committee, who also knew Diem, angrily remarked: "This act of assassination is repulsive... The military junta which now rules Viet Nam has not shown itself to be any less ruthless or any less autocratic than the former regime..." (The new junta has dissolved the national assembly.)

America, said Zablocki, "gave encouragement to the coup. And if we knew of it, but failed to exert pressure to ensure Diem's safe conduct," said Zablocki, "the shadow of blame falls on our nation."

On several occasions during Diem's last months in power, U.S. Embassy officials granted asylum to Diem's enemies. But after Diem was overthrown, when his brother Ngo Dinh Can sought asylum, we refused, and turned him over to the mercies of the revolutionaries.

Nor has the overthrow of Diem brought an end to "Buddhist" intrigue and suicides. By December 3rd, 1963, three such self-immolations had taken place. But unlike the earlier anti-Diem actions, these were given little publicity or attention. Anti-Diem reporters, who had shed crocodile tears about harsh treatment meted out to Diem's enemies, were too busy trying to "get" General Paul Harkins, and initiate witch hunts against others—both American and Vietnamese—who recognized Diem's qualities and respected him.

"Has the press corps covering the Viet Nam war lit a time bomb that may explode in disaster within one to five years?"

That question was raised recently by Frank Conniff, national editor of Hearst Newspapers.

Mr. Coniff returned recently from the sixth task force trip undertaken by William Randolph Hearst, Jr. and Bob Considine since 1955. They stopped in Saigon for an interview with the then President Ngo Dinh Diem. Also in the group was Warren Rogers, chief Washington correspondent for Hearst Headline Service. The plane on which he was a passenger was hit by Viet Cong bullets just before it landed in Saigon.

Mr. Conniff said he agreed with the view of Assistant Secretary of State Robert Manning that when the full Viet Nam story is written "it will be clear that—for good or ill—the press had a major share in the outcome.

"There is no doubt that the American reporter played an influential role in the dramatic military coup last week," Mr. Conniff said. "It was mainly in setting the climate in Washington and in Viet Nam.

"Now who knows what will be the outcome? It may well be that a time bomb has been lit that will explode in disaster in one, two, three or five years."

The Hearst group also disagreed on the emphasis being put by some correspondents —specifically David Halberstam of the *New York Times* - on religious aspects of Viet Nam's crisis. The fact that President Diem was a Catholic and seventy per cent of the population was non-Catholic was not so important as it has been made out to be, in Mr. Conniff's opinion. He considered politics more critical than religion.

Mr. Conniff said:

> My main comment on the Saigon press corps is regarding their lack of skepticism, the sort that comes from long experience. I wonder what they think now of a new regime that begins with three murders — President Diem, his brother, Ngo Dinh Nhu, and Navy Commander Capt. Ho Tan Quyen — abolishment of a good constitution, and a manifesto that says a free press is needed as a guide to democracy. Surely the correspondents must agree that the duty of a free press is to inform and reveal, not to guide.

Will David Halberstam, young, twentyish, *New York Times'* correspondent, be rated the Herbert Matthews of South Viet Nam? These reporters, it is now being claimed, helped ignite the revolutions in Saigon and Havana, respectively.

Matthews literally generated world pressures against Batista in Cuba after a series of exclusive interviews with Fidel Castro in early 1957. His highly favorable portrayal of the Cuban Communist created a climate of opinion through which supporters of Castro, particularly in the

U.S. State Department, could happily construct plots which played a major role in destroying Batista's anti-Communist regime.

Similarly, Halberstam's severely critical accounts of the Diem Government in South Vietnam enabled the anti-Diem faction in the State Department to rise to power. As anti-Diem opinion mounted in this country and around the world, the Department implemented a series of crushing economic and military measures against South Viet Nam, thus feeding the growing anti-Diem sentiment there which eventually exploded in the form of the bloody coup d'etat. (Halberstam, it is interesting to note, was so trusted by the enemies of Diem that he received the pre-arranged signal for the coup the night before.)

That Matthews misjudged Castro is history. What will eventually happen in Vietnam is uncertain. It is disquieting, however, to know that the *Times,* which so often foretells governmental policies, has now called for Vietnam's "neutralization," an idea which the murdered Diem had determinedly opposed.

No one has ever believed that under Diem's regime there was democracy, or even, except a few Vietnamese intellectuals, that democracy was desirable. Communism had to be beaten, and for that the little-comprehended idea of democracy was too weak a weapon.

One South Vietnamese who would call himself an intellectual said in the quiet that followed the shelling that South Vietnam was not yet ready, and indeed had no preparation, for democracy. When one then asked, "What was the revolution for?" the answer was "It was for the Americans," and one was back on familiar Asian ground. The outsider can't deny that the Americans — and the British — wanted a change of government, but he wonders whether any of the parties concerned had a clear idea of what was coming.

The Buddhist leadership in South Vietnam, according to South Vietnamese police records, which Americans do not dispute, is thoroughly permeated by communism. But the funeral pyres of Buddhist priests were more than American public opinion could take.

The American embassy in Saigon, followed faithfully by the British, supported Diem's regime until the realization came that the Buddhist suicides were, as presented in the world's press, revolting world opinion.

It is true enough that those monks focused attention on public discontent in South Vietnam, and thus acted as a catalyst for troublemakers far outside the Buddhist fold. But the discontent was there before, while the Western powers were silently acquiescent.

Yet the Americans, at the very least, were tacit partners in the coup, with the British running happily behind. Almost every army unit that moved up to fire at the Presidential Palace automatically had American officers and NCOs attached. The Americans, at least in an advisory capacity, assisted in the attack on the palace simply because they were so attached.

There were no orders given, as there were, for example, to British officers in India and Pakistan in 1947 that they should resign in case of battle. It was, indeed, on American military advice that the Vietnamese corps were altered, thus making it possible for the Third Corps to take part in the revolt.

All this having been said, there was clearly a time when the rebellion might have failed.

The marines set things aright by taking over the post office and broadcasting station, and the air force, long known for its antagonism towards Diem, was willing to fire rockets in the direction of the palace even if it failed to hit it, but Big Minh hesitated. When he came in, Diem's regime was over, but clearly he had been more hesitant than the Americans in wishing it so.

It is interesting to note that the far right as well as the left hated Diem and attacked him during his lifetime. It wasn't only the Communists and left-liberals, but also Merwin K. Hart, Hilaire du Berrier, the H. L. Hunt radio program and *American Opinion* who constantly berated him.

It may be early to attempt a definitive appraisal of the Diem administration in South Vietnam. It is not too early to identify the cynical propaganda with which those who betrayed him seek to exculpate their guilt.

President Ngo Dinh Diem was a man of exemplary character, of selfless devotion to his country, of deep humanity. The campaign of vilification had to be made of whole cloth.

According to General Thomas A. Lane,

> The scheme was designed by the Communists with consummate skill. President Diem was vulnerable in being a Catholic, a minority religion in the country. He was doubly vulnerable in depending for support upon a Catholic president of the United States. The communists shrewdly figured that the American president could not support President Diem in a conflict with another religious group, whatever the merits of the issue might be.
>
> They had at hand the means for the

job. In the war with France, the communist leader Ho-Chi-Minh had found the Buddhist robes a convenient cover for his agents. He had bonzes planted in South Vietnam where they could stir up religious conflict. They dominated the Buddhist Association, a new organization, which represented about eight per cent of the Vietnamese population.

After the initial rioting at Hue in May, President Diem sought to resolve the complaints. He found that the Buddhist Association leaders were determined to overthrow his government. There was no middle ground on which the complaints could be adjudicated. Diem was destroyed because the U.S. government would not support his rejection of the impossible demands of the Buddhist Association.

One measure of President Diem is that all his enemies are alive. When air force rebels in 1960 bombed his palace into such a shambles that he had to abandon it, one of the guilty pilots was captured. Obviously, a trial would require conviction and execution of the lieutenant. The president never brought the young man to trial. Diem refused to take a life for political reasons, even for rebellion.

With everyone else in Saigon knowing of the conspiracy of his officers, President Diem must have had information of it. Perhaps he refused to believe that these men whom he had appointed to their high positions could be so mad. Caesar made the same mistake. Perhaps he could not believe that the U.S. would promote such betrayal. He did not realize that a Catholic president of the U.S. would not support what was right and just.

History will show that President Diem
was too humane and charitable to survive
in the climate of power in 1963. He was
not ruthless enough to arrest and execute
the military conspirators and replace them
with loyal men. He tried too long to
placate the implacable Buddhist Association. He would not even deport the mis-
guided American reporters who were his
bitter enemies. He tried instead to concil-
iate and resolve differences without the
harsh measures so necessary to the survival of his government but so foreign
to his character. His mildness encouraged
rebellion.

President Diem has been replaced by
more ruthless men who, like Castro, do
not hesitate to execute their prisoners. The
propaganda stories that Diem and Nhu
committed suicide are transparent fraud.
They were executed by an officer dis-
patched from headquarters; and an officer
sent to bring in important prisoners does
not execute them unless he has been told
to do so.

Ngo Dinh Diem was a product of the
highest culture and ideals of the West,
striving to make his vision real for the
Vietnamese people. He was the victim of
sordid aspects of western civilization which
he did not know.

One incident which occurred after the coup
shed retrospective light on the degree of Ambassador Lodge's responsibility, namely the surrender of Diem's brother, Ngo Dinh Can. Seeing
that the battle was lost, Can, who lived near
Hue, requested sanctuary from the Canadian
Redemptorist Fathers. The Fathers, seeking
fuller security for Can, turned in good faith to

the American Consul in Hue, who, in turn, referred the matter to the U.S. Embassy in Saigon. The Embassy assured the security of Can and sent a U.S. military plane to take him to "a safe place." But when the plane landed in Saigon, Mr. Can was turned over to the mercies of the revolutionary junta.

Ngo Dinh Nhu, said of the Ambassador:

> Lodge never stopped working against us, with the cocksureness that a representative of a colonial power might have evinced, thirty years ago, toward a protectorate. Although President Diem did his best to show Lodge that the game he played led only to favoring Communism, Diem's remarks left the Ambassador quite cold. Do you know that Lodge had the cheek to request my wife's departure and my own? Just as if our Vietnamese Ambassador in Washington had requested President Kennedy to order his brother Robert and his sister-in-law to leave the United States. From what we hear, Lodge does not bother with the normal business of an Ambassador, which would be to galvanize the American forces sent here to give us a good hand and to strengthen the friendship between our two governments. No. His only care is to intrigue against the *legal government* to which he has been accredited.[1]

The generals who took part in the coup did so because of American incitement, which led the generals to feel, as did the students, that they were in tune with world opinion, and would receive the applause of the leaders of the free

[1] Labin, *op. cit.,* p. 35.

world. "Who could have resisted the enormous temptation thus offered which amalgamated, as the prize of the coup: *Power,* monetary *affluence,* the *favor* of United States authorities with consequent recovery of economic *aid,* and finally world *applause.*[2]

Much before the first insignificant wave of demonstrations in favor of the coup, there had been another wave of obviously organized bands, Communist-inspired, prepared to launch its campaign of violence and terror. Fifteen minutes after the last shot was fired, at 7 a.m. November 2nd, Miss Labin observed disciplined groups, marching in order: "They went straight to the houses of the most active anti-Communists and burned them. They sacked all the centers of anti-Communism, such as bookshops, libraries, newspapers, and information centers. Even some establishments which had absolutely no connection with Diem, such as the building in which the Asian Peoples Anti-Communist League held its congress--at which foreign participants, while anti-Communist, had no ties with the Diem government--were put to the torch... Then, an hour later, some of the groups which perpetrated these raids started shouting Communist slogans: 'Down with the strategic hamlets!' 'Unity with the North!' 'Stop the war!'[3]

The most peculiar aspect of the whole affair was the failure of the world press to publish pictures of these scenes of looting and burning, a large number of which were taken by several journalists in Saigon.

[2]*Ibid.,* p. 36.
[3]*Ibid.,* pp. 37, 38.

CHAPTER TWELVE
THE DECLINE SINCE DIEM

The Decline Since Diem

Few people took notice of a single pistol shot in a Saigon backyard about 9 o'clock the night of January 31, 1964.   There was general relief that a coup d'etat had been accomplished the day before without bloodshed; compared with the battle to oust President Diem three months earlier, General Khanh's accession to power was virtually painless.

The man who died was Nguyen Van Nhung, a 44 year old major in the Vietnamese Army with more than 20 years of service. He was not well known except as a loyal aide for his entire army career to Major General Duong Van Minh, "Big Minh," who stepped into power as the leader of the military junta the day of Mr. Diem's downfall.

To a small group of people involved on both sides of the November coup, however, Major Nhung had become a symbol. He was the man credited, or blamed, for killing President Diem, and Ngo Dinh Nhu, his brother, the morning of November 2, while his chief was strengthening the army's position as the head of the revolutionary government.

Major Nhung had killed President Diem.

Then the major himself was dead, either a suicide in captivity or murdered by an unknown hand. Why was this little known major the sole victim of General Khanh's coup d'etat?

Two important men asked this question. One was General Minh himself, despairing, according to his confidants, at the loss of a faithful aide.

The other important man who wondered about Major Nhung's death was a man of religion, a Buddhist bonze, or monk, for whom things had not gone well since the Buddhist uprisings that had led to Mr. Diem's ouster and death.

This bonze was in the process of gathering funds to go abroad, to leave Vietnam and to "bury his life" as he told his few intimates. Hearing of Major Nhung's death, his ambitions for political power revived and he canceled his travel plans.

The fear of both these men was that Major Nhung had died in the settlement of an old score, that with General Khanh's accession to power the partisans of Mr. Diem were given their chance to avenge the President's death.

In the months that followed and even still today, General Khanh was unable to dispel the notion that somehow his Government was serving as the cover for a revival of pro-Diem forces.

At his first news conference, on January 3, the new leader dealt at length with his role in an attempted coup in November, 1960, when as a young brigadier, he was believed to have saved President Diem's life.

General Khanh insisted that his role had been merely one of mediator to help moderate that crisis. Yet afterward President Diem gave him command of troops in the then critical Second Army Corps region in central Vietnam.

Repeatedly General Khanh had denied adherence to the Can Lao or "Personalist" party led by Mr. Nhu. As for the people around him, the general could not deny that many army officers in high positions had served in responsible jobs under Mr. Diem, perhaps had even been members of the Can Lao.

But General Khanh said, if all the Government employees of the nine years of Mr. Diem's rule were eliminated from service, few with experience would be left to run the complicated affairs of administration.

But fears lingered among certain civilian politicians, among the Buddhists and among both groups' army adherents. These fears flared to the surface in September 1964 when Khanh was forced to step down.

General Khanh had moved quickly to set up his Government in the first two weeks of February 1964. His intention was to rely heavily on civilian politicians, representatives of old-time nationalist political parties banned under Mr. Diem. As one senior diplomat said: "Khanh wanted to have different shades of opinion in his Government-well, he got them, with disastrous results."

Chief among the returned exiles was a deceptively mild and unassuming man named Nguyen Ton Hoan, leader of the predominant faction of the old Dai Viet, or Greater Vietnam Movement. Mr. Hoan closed his Vietnamese restaurant on the Left Bank in Paris to return to Saigon after a nine year absence.

He did so expecting to be Premier, for some of his army contacts in the Dai Viet, a nationalist party, had been with General Khanh from the start of the planning for the January 1964 coup.

General Khanh saw, however, that rivalry and infighting among the splintered political parties was so great that one faction could gain support from the others. The general became Premier himself, leaving to Mr. Hoan the post of First Deputy Premier.

It was still a post from which the Dai Viet thought it could extend its party power. Government appointments promptly were handed out to party regulars and General Khanh found himself having to spend as much time holding reins on Mr. Hoan as he did in fighting the war — the activity he said he really wanted to pursue. Early in April, the general succeeded in squeezing out one of the main Dai Viet manipulators, Ha Thuc Ky, Interior Minister, who had tried to put party members in key jobs of province chiefs.

With Mr. Hoan's resignation, the uncomfortable alliance of General Khanh and the Dai Viet was finally broken. For the first seven months, the army was at once General Khanh's greatest strength and his major burden. He succeeded in splitting potential enemies, a signal achievement in itself, with the help of certain colleagues tied to him by one means or another.

By his side, though not always on his side, was Maj. General Tran Thien Khiem, Defense Minister and commander in chief of the armed forces. If any coup were to have been pulled off, General Khiem's adherence would have been crucial. It was eagerly sought by the Dai Viet in particular, informed sources said.

But General Khiem apparently stood by his

military school classmate, though General Khanh had to promote the silent, humorless Khiem to the rank of lieutenant general, meaning that General Khiem outranks both Generals Khanh and Minh.

Across the country side General Khanh moved to put his own key men in key command positions as much as possible. Provincial chiefs, field commanders and staff officers became the general's backbone of local support — he had little among the population.

The resulting dislocation, following so soon the first junta's changes after Mr. Diem, aroused concern among Vietnamese and American officers alike. But General Khanh maintained that it was the only way to insure effective control over the war effort. Americans reluctantly saw his point and eventually the command structure was stabilized.

General Minh remained a central problem. The husky and slow-moving officer seemed to do little during General Khanh's seven month tenure though he was retained in the honorific role of head of state.

One day, in a good mood, General Minh dropped in unannounced at General Khanh's office where the Premier was poring through stocks of daily governmental papers. The senior general sat at his side and helped him for the morning. General Khanh was so delighted he talked about it for days afterward. But it never seemed to happen again.

Persons close to General Minh say he never got over Major Nhung's death; the major's portrait still hangs over a private Buddhist shrine in the general's staff office.

Perhaps it was because he could not forgive

the man he held responsible for his faithful aide's death, perhaps it was because General Khanh had arrested General Minh's colleagues in the first junta, perhaps it was because he saw General Khanh as only a brash upstart-probably for all three reasons prestigious "Big Minh" refused to lift a finger on General Khanh's behalf.

Premier Khanh had other trump cards, however. He was clever and energetic, willing to work harder than any general the Vietnamese had seen in recent years. He seemed not to mind responsibility, though he asserted that he followed a majority vote of his mixed civilian-military Cabinet on most policy decisions.

Furthermore, General Khanh had the personal support of the United States from the day Secretary of Defense Robert S. McNamara threw his arm around the beaming general and shouted to a crowd "Vietnam Moun nam!" ("Long live Vietnam!")

American aid was increased — it is now approaching $2 million a day — and Mr. McNamara promised Premier Khanh "a blank check." United States military personnel, who someone had said, would be phased out by the end of the next year were increased, now totaling 18,000 men in that country.

With Premier Khanh, many Americans began to hope. In a more honest and open atmosphere than the year before there was little downright optimism, but good things started to happen. Plans to pacify the country were agreed upon and Americans considered them good plans. The army performed well against the Vietcong, sometimes.

In July, things began going wrong. Military

progress in the field was all but wiped out by a Vietcong offensive before the rainy season. The insurgents' build-up during the quiet months of spring gave them a capacity to strike hard at widely separated points, keeping the initiative from more unwieldy Government forces.

General Khanh grew openly tired of the pacification strategy and his responses to American pressure became more reluctant as he saw that this method of fighting could not work fast enough to keep the population from growing restive under the increased demands of war.

Picking up public hints of American policy makers, Premier Khanh came out in July for an expansion of the effort and attacks on Communist North Vietnam, the command point of the Vietcong insurgency. In advocating his "march to the North," General Khanh acknowledged later, he did so against the advice of his Cabinet-one of the only two times he said he had acted like a dictator.

American policy-makers apparently did not mean for their hints to be taken literally at that time. As Premier Khanh saw it, his staunch friends the Americans had slapped him down and he was left alone to face new threats and a war in the countryside that apparently could not be won.

A stroke of luck for him was the North Vietnamese attacks on United States destroyers in the Gulf of Tonkin and the retaliatory United States air strike early in August. Premier Khanh grasped at a last straw and rushed into new actions that brought everything to a tragic climax.

Meanwhile, another element had been at work. The Buddhists of South Vietnam, five million of whom are said to practice the religion, had shown their force during their six-month protest that led to the downfall of the Diem Government, which they accused of favoring the Catholic minority.

After the November revolution they seemed to fade away from active participation in politics. They appeared to be torn by internal dissension and incapable of any united movement such as they had launched against Mr. Diem; presumably the leaders were quietly at work trying to set up tight organization over the sects of Vietnamese Buddhism.

On January 3, a unified Buddhist organization came into being. Religious and secular affairs were clearly separated with the highly centralized secular affairs section being organized into a cabinet resembling a shadow government. Vietnamese Buddhism had never advanced so boldly into temporal affairs before. The man who drafted the new Buddhist charter, confidently expecting to become a sort of Buddhist Premier was none other than Thich Tri Quang.

With the formation of a unified Buddhist organization based on 11 of the country's 14 sects, elections were held for key posts, but when the votes were counted Tri Quang found himself defeated. The direction of Buddhist secular affairs went instead to Thich Tam Chau, a refugee from North Vietnam. Tri Quang was despondent. He told friends he was going to make a pilgrimage to India, Ceylon and Japan to "bury his life."

Meantime Tam Chau organized the Buddhist structure, and a shadow government took on substance. Now there were seven senior monks, each controlling affairs in several provinces, roughly comparable to the Government's four army corps commanders. Each province has one Buddhist representative and two deputies comparable to the Government's province chief and deputies. All these field officials are appointed by and are responsible to the Buddhist cabinet, the Secular Affairs Institute.

When General Khan seized power January 30, 1964, Tam Chau threw Buddhist support to the new government. But Tri Quang had other ideas. The continuation in power of some Diem aides and the shooting of Major Nhung gave him rope for a resumed campaign of the Buddhist Left. He abruptly changed his travel plans, and moved to Hue to prepare for a new bid for power. He may have instigated some of the religious riots in central Vietnam. He certainly took these occasions to stir up anti-Catholic hatreds, and direct them against Catholic (Can Lao) influences in the Kanh Government. He returned to Saigon, and apparently sold some of Tam Chau's followers on the need for "vigilance" and a united front against alleged Catholics in the Government who were, he claimed, striving to revive Diem's "anti-Buddhism." Tri Quang's target was now the Kanh Government itself, which, he had persuaded most influential Buddhists, was just Diem under different colors. [1]

General Kanh, according to reliable sources, saw the United States air strikes on North Vietnam as the excuse he needed to usher in emergency decrees tightening his authority over the divisive elements that had been troubling him. This he did on August 7.

[1] *New York Times,* September 4, 1964, p. 8.

But imbued with the American ideas of a strong war government, he went further. Nine days later the Premier forced through a drastic new Constitution, installing himself, as President, ousting General Minh, abandoning the Military Revolutionary Council and assuming virtually dictatorial powers.

The Buddhists saw the pretext they had been seeking: for their part, Dai Viet adherents, fearing they were being edged out, unleashed their student supporters to denounce General Khanh's moves. The Buddhists did the same.

Then General Khanh and his aides made a risky decision. Aware of the dangers of looking like a new Diem, General Khanh ordered the law enforcement authorities not to resist the agitators in the streets.

"Let them demonstrate," a Khanh aide said. "They will quickly see that we are not repressing them."

But as General Khanh acknowledged, "We believed it was a small-scale movement — only later did we see it was a vast movement across the country."

Banner-waving demonstrators turned to violence against a radio station and the Ministry of Information. In centers of tension such as Danang, long-simmering Buddhist-Catholic hatreds flared into a fury of street fighting. Abruptly, the Vietcong leadership reduced its terrorism and attacks in the provinces, according to field reports, and sent trained agitators by the busload into Saigon.

Beginning on August 27th, witnesses saw country buses full of young men but no women driving to the central market square, where the Buddhists had demonstrated earlier. The Buddhist ceremony had broken down into an unofficial gathering of backstreet youths. The new arrivals disappeared into the crowd, the independent witnesses said, and by the 28th, the market square was barricaded against the police. It took a military and police assault to clear up pockets of defiance. The Government troops fired shots — mostly into the air—but there were deaths and the hope of building popular support through leniency was lost.

General Khanh had already capitulated. Late the 31st, he met with Thich Tam Chau and Thich Tri Quang to try to reach a settlement. Almost point by point a communique he issued when he stepped down answered the Buddhists' demands that the August 16 Constitution be revoked, that action be taken against "impure" Diemist remnants and that preparations be made for a government more favorable to Buddhism.

The author of these demands was Tri Quang. According to reliable sources, he drafted them on rough sheets of paper in his air-conditioned room in a pagoda the previous evening.

The emergence of organized Buddhism as an unabashed political power in South Vietnam offers little promise of security for the Government of Vietnam. As one Western diplomat in Saigon has reportedly remarked: "If we won a clear-cut military victory against the Communist guerrillas, we could still lose this country in five minutes through subversion." And the instrument of subversion would be the increasingly powerful Buddhist organization.

It is no longer only the supporters of the late Ngo Dinh Diem who suspect the motives behind Buddhist anti-government protests made —for the past year—against "religious discrimination." According to Beverly Deepe, special correspondent of the *New York Herald Tribune,* such statements as the following can be heard from the lips of Western diplomats, members of the foreign press corps and Vietnamese themselves in Saigon:

> It's stupid to ask if the Buddhist leaders are Communist or not. You have only to check the policy they are following. The Communists have infiltrated the Buddhist Movement... If we do not put them back into a position as a religion and keep them out of politics, we will never finish with them. I am not ashamed to say I was wrong. I was for the Buddhists last year when they were fighting Ngo Dinh Diem and his family... But now I think the Communists have infiltrated at all levels.
>
> The record of the Buddhists over the past year is stepping from one slippery stone to another, jockeying for position. They've taken advantage of every concession the government made them and each of their final agreements has been broken the next day.[2]

At the beginning of November, 1964, the country embarked on its third government since the Diem period ended in November, 1963. During the spring and early summer the dissatisfied religious and political elements in the country were relatively quiescent. But their agitation in the streets of Saigon and other cities turned the last days of August into what an American general called an "agony" from which anti-Communist forces barely recovered.

After that it took two months for a successor regime to emerge.

[2]*America,* September 19, 1964, p. 286-7.

To Tran Van Huong, the new Premier, fell the responsibility of forging a new Government administration, virtually from top to bottom. He was working against the relentless pressure of a highly organized insurgent machine.

Between January and October 1964 nearly 500 Government officials were kidnapped by Vietcong terrorists in the villages, roughly comparable to American townships, and in the hamlets, the cluster of homes where peasants live. Almost the same number were assassinated.

Intelligence analysts suspect that many of the kidnapped officials are put through indoctrination courses and possibly sent back to insurgent areas to administer them for the Vietcong.

Communist insurgents are spreading terror now in areas of the countryside and in cities that they could not penetrate before. Officials find themselves unable to visit districts that the Government once controlled.

The United States effort in South Vietnam was itself the target of a bold Communist attack on the anniversary of Mr. Diem's downfall. Mortar shelling of the top-security airport of Bienhoa, with the loss of four American lives and the destruction of six American B-57 jet bombers, was vivid evidence of the increasing vulnerability of United States forces as the Communists acquire access to more areas of the country.

Loyal officials in hamlets and villages are being assassinated or kidnapped at the rate of eighty to one-hundred a month, according to official statistics.

Thus three years after the United States dramatically enlarged its commitment to South Vietnam, Communist pressures and the weakness of the Government have once again brought the country to the brink of collapse.

Once again many American and Vietnamese officials are thinking of new, enlarged commitments — this time to carry the conflict beyond the frontiers of South Vietnam.[3]

But as political instability continued, featured by the persistent influence of General Kanh, romantic American insistence on civilian government, and irresponsible Buddhist and student attacks on *any* anti-Communist administration, many observers of the Vietnamese scene recalled the comparative stability and determination of the Ngo Dinh Diem regime. And for those involved in the tragedy of November, 1963, the haunting memory of the Last of the Mandarins lingers on.

[3]*New York Times,* November 2, 1964, p. 18.

APPENDIX

THE PHILOSOPHY OF
PRESIDENT NGO DINH DIEM

The Philosophy of
President Ngo Dinh Diem

If the man shapes events, history also shapes the man who is receptive to its influence. President Diem's family background and the effect of the teachings of his formative years - during a period of the first importance in his country's history - are factors which help one to understand in some measure the development of thought which has produced a personality which is widely considered to be one of the most significant in South-East Asia. [1]

The President's early years were spent in the atmosphere of guidance which his father, a Counsellor and Minister of Emperor Thanh-Thai, exercised over a large number of the thinkers of his time. Apart from being the initiator of a modern system of education, His Excellency Ngo-Dinh Kha was the adviser of a galaxy of important figures. One notable instance of his foresight was the creation of a National College which acted as a symbol of Western modernization brought to Viet Nam. Although he felt that the time was not ripe for revolution—

[1] Sirdar Ikbal Ali Shah, *Vietnam* (London: Octagon Press, 1960), p. 119.

education would bring evolution as things were then moving—he was able to give them the benefit of his experience. As in the case of all Oriental families, his father gave him a thorough grounding in the spiritual and cultural aspects of his heritage. He was sent to a college where he received a Western as well as a Vietnamese education.

First and foremost, the President felt that the destiny as well as the roots of the country were grounded and nurtured by the Asian heritage. "What makes the destiny of Asia so tragic?" he asked, perhaps rhetorically, when addressing the National Assembly of another Far Eastern country. As he saw it, the tragedy lay in the necessity of fighting a new enemy: after Colonialism, Communism, the new form of imperialism. This diagnosis is one which shows how conscious he was of the unity of Asia. It also reveals that he was a realist as well as an idealist.

For centuries, as President Diem has remarked, "the social life of Viet Nam has been based upon a federation of villages whose business has been conducted by the people of the villages."

This system worked smoothly, thanks to the strong spirit of unity to be found everywhere in the countryside. The unity was based upon the family, upon the rights and the duties of the individual within the family, which, in turn, respected his identity. There is much in the thinking of other places and other cultures, he stated, which can with advantage be grafted upon Asian thinking. Following the decision that there was room for a nationally integrated synthesis of all that was advantageous, he had ploughed an almost lone furrow in earlier days, when he sought to assimilate only the best of the Western thinking with the priceless heritage of the East.

He recognized to the full that Asia was in the process of passing from the old to the new; but he believed that with modernity there is a very great deal in Asian culture that can and must be retained. In no sense was he a fatalist who says that the ancient Asian civilizations must be submerged in those of the West:

> It is obvious that we must not allow fatalism and defeatism to overwhelm us. Neither must we be deluded into adopting seemingly easy solutions which consist in blindly imitating Western methods. Asia, in fact, must not copy the West, because things that are copied are never assimilated into the body politic of any civilisation.

When the President declared that "the technical effectiveness represented by Communism exercises a great temptation to the Asian masses," he was in reality pointing out that it might take more time under freedom for his liberal policies to bear fruit. He was fully alive to the fact that the yearning desire for haste in the minds of the myriad could put an enormous pressure upon Asian leaders, quite regardless of their ideologies.

> Fortunately for South Viet Nam, and for the liberal-mindedness of its leaders, there is always the awful example of the Communist-held lands north of the 17th parallel to deter those who would display impatience. On their very doorstep they can see the fruits of totalitarianism - and its cost. [2]

[2]*Ibid.,* p. 121.

Against highly-propagandised totalitarianism, President Ngo Dinh Diem had to extol the benefits (which could not later accrue) of a democratic way of life. And democracy, as he saw it, is not so much a matter of mere laws and texts, but rather in essence a state of mind and a way of living in which the primary axiom is the utmost respect to all human beings.

Cut right back to its essentials, the philosophy of Ngo-Dinh Diem was a spiritual one, in expression as in basis. Thus it was that he was able to say, in his Message to the National Assembly on the foundation of the Constitution in 1956: "The basis for democracy can only be a spiritual one."

What does this mean, and how is it related to Asian thought? The fundamental spirit of democracy, as has been noted, has been present in Asian thought for countless centuries. The President recognized this in another address, when he postulated: "The traditional notion of the transcendence of the human soul is glimpsed by Indian speculation; there is the equality of all men preached by Buddhism; there is the freedom born of the spontaneous emergence of Taoist being; and the cosmic and individual virtues of Confucian Jen and of the Kien-Ngai of Motsu."

This is the kernel of his philosophy, and one which he was determined to bring out into the light of day. Speaking with the clarity of vision which marked him out even among progressive Asian thinkers, he told the Indian Council of World Affairs in New Delhi in 1957:

Asians lost sight of this vital current in their tradition... For... does not our spirituality, of which we are so proud, simply conceal a narrow conservatism and a form

of escapism from concrete responsibilities?
... Has not Buddhist compassion become a
pretext for not practising justice which
must precede all charity?... And is not
tolerance, which so many can mistake for
freedom, the result of paternalistic indul-
gence?

In brief, President Ngo-Dinh Diem had little
time either for those leaning"forward"to totalitarianism, or the aculturists, eternally leaning back-
wards. He was seeking a real, palpable re-
nascence in Asia. He believed that this could
be brought about by going back to the truly
authentic sources of Eastern thought; and, at the
same time, drawing "inspiration from the permanent values of Western culture to provide statesmen with guiding principles in their efforts to
solve the problems of Asia." To this he has
added, on another occasion: "Do not the forces
of Western technique which we so much despise
and which others admire without reservation,
contain a creative spirit which justifies them?"
He once pointed out to his people in this
context that the "technical knowledge of Europe
is not the property of Europe alone. It belongs
to humanity in its entirety." Yet he was always
fully alive to the dangers of uncritical and indiscriminate acceptance of the principles of
Western technology; if only because he never
allowed himself to forget that eight-tenths of his
people derive their livelihood from the land.
He had no wish to see the rapid changes of
Japan reproduced in Vietnam. In his mind, the
vast alterations in the structure of the Japanese
economy brought few benefits to the individual.
There is a very close affinity between Pandit
Nehru's "Basic Approach" and the thinking of

President Ngo-Dinh Diem. Each of these Asian leaders was a staunch nationalist, poles apart from that of Communist or even European nationalism. It will have been noted that both leaders, while stressing the importance of their ancient cultures, are fully alive to the fact that the best of the West has to be assimilated.

The philosophy of President Diem has already produced good results in his own country; in reality it contains a message to entire awakening Asia; for the introduction of what is known as the ideals of Personalism and the universal value of freedom are quite unique in our own day. They are unique not in the sense that the philosophy is a new one, but its practical application to modern times is the need of the hour. It is undoubtedly an answer to the urge of Communism which is fast sweeping South-East Asia, and has made its appearance in other parts of the East.

To deny the existence of God — as do the Communists — is to deny the immortality of the human soul. This in turn is tantamount to denying the spiritual character of true freedom, which constitutes its essence and gives man his transcendent value. This love of freedom stemming as it does from the spiritual mandates, and which is opposed to merely material 'freedom' is symbolic of what is projected as Personalism. [3]

The ideals thus set by President Diem have now become the national ideals of the entire South Vietnamese people, for he helped inject into the people that intrinsic value which spiritual standards impart to the activities of an awakened

[3] *Ibid.,* p. 126.

nation. The freedom, or Personalism, of which he speaks, brings man nearer to that perfection which mankind is seeking; he feels that real freedom means the independence of mind, which can only be brought about by a hard struggle against materialistic forces, which imprison conscience and destroy man's personality and his dignity. Personalism, thus could form the essential foundation of the ideological front of the Asian, or indeed all god-fearing people everywhere if the menace of godlessness - as freely expressed by the Communist ideals - can be combated and overpowered. Personalism, therefore, is a spiritual revolution by which the Communist or any other godless idea might be counter-acted.

Democracy, he (Diem) holds, is a form of regime in which the people's authority is supreme; and Personalism is a system based on the divine, therefore, spiritual law, which applied to a regime, extols man's transcendent value; Personalism, thus, being a direct and primordial factor enobles all political actions because benefiting from the Divine spark, it gives it that permanency which other factors cannot give. Democracy, based on people's views is liable to change due to elasticity inherent in it; and deprived of its spiritual ingredient, it might even degenerate into materialism; not so Personalism. The practice of Personalism is symbolic of good citizenship with a highly developed civic spirit. It can, therefore, be said that Personalism constitutes the very soul of freedom within democracy; without it there can be no true freedom.[4]

[4]*Ibid.*, p. 127.

BIBLIOGRAPHY

American Friends of Vietnam, *America's Stake in Vietnam.* New York, Carnegie Press, 1956.

Amoureux, Henri, *Croix sur l'Indochine.* Paris, Domat, 1955.

Buttinger, Joseph, *The Smaller Dragon, A Political History of Vietnam.* New York, Praeger, 1958.

Catroux, Georges, *Deux actes du drame indochinois.* Paris, Plon, 1959.

Chesneauz, Jean, *Contribution a l'histoire de la nation vietnamienne.* Paris, Editions Sociales, 1956.

Cole, Allan B., ed., *Conflict in Indo-China and International Repercussions.* New York, Cornell University Press, 1956.

Decoux, Jean, *A la Barre de l'Indochine.* Paris, Plon, 1949.

Devillers, Philippe, *Histoire du Vietnam de 1940 a 1952.* Paris, Editions du Seuil, 1952.

Fall, Bernard, ed., *The Two Vietnams.* New York, Praeger, 1963.

Fifield, Russell H., *The Diplomacy of Southeast Asia:* 1945-1948. New York, Harper, 1958.

Fishel, Wesley, *Problems of Freedom: Vietnam.* Glencoe, Free Press, 1961.

Hammer, Ellen J., *The Struggle for Indo-China.* Stanford, Stanford University Press, 1954.

Holland, William L., *Asian Nationalism and the West*. New York, Macmillan, 1953.

Huard, Pierre, and Durand, Maurice, *Connaissance du Viet-Nam*. Paris, Imprimerie Nationale, 1954.

Khoi, Le Thanh, *Le Viet-Nam, Histoire et civilisation*. Paris, Editions de Minuit, 1955.

Labin, Suzanne, *Vietnam, An Eye-Witness Account*. Springfield, Va., Crestwood Books, 1964.

Lancaster, Donald, *The Emancipation of French Indochina*. London, Oxford University Press, 1961.

Lindholm, Richard, ed., *Vietnam, The First Five Years*. Ann Arbor, University of Michigan Press, 1959.

Marchand, Jean, *Le Drame indochinois*. Paris, Peyronnet, 1953.

Masson, Andre, *Histoire du Vietnam*. Paris, Presses Universitaires de France, 1960.

Mus, Paul, *Vietnam: Sociologie d'une guerre*. Paris, Editions du Seuil, 1952.

Mus, Paul, *Le Viet-Nam chez lui*. Paris, Centre d'Etudes de Politique Etrangere, 1946.

Rowan, Carl T., *The Pitiful and the Proud*. New York, Random House, 1956.

Savani, A.M., *Visages et images du sud Viet-Nam*. Saigon, 1955.

Sirdar Ikbal Ali Shah, *Vietnam*. London, Octagon Press, 1960.

U.S. Senate Foreign Relations Committee, *Report by Senator Mike Mansfield on a Study Mission to Vietnam, Cambodia, Laos*. Washington, GPO, 1954.

Vandenbosch, Amry, and Butwell, Richard A., *Southeast Asia Among the World Powers*. Lexington, University of Kentucky Press, 1957.

Werth, Alexander, *La France depuis la guerre, 1944-57*. Paris, Gallimard, 1931.